LOOSE ON LIQUIDATORS

The Role of a Liquidator in a Voluntary Winding-Up

2nd Edition

Michael Crystal LL.B., B.C.L.,
of the Middle Temple, Barrister,
and John Higham M.A., LL.B.,
of Lincoln's Inn, Barrister

Jordan & Sons Limited
Bristol

ISBN 0 85308 064 X ✓

First Edition 1972
Second Edition 1981

Published by
Jordan & Sons Limited
PO Box 260
15 Pembroke Road
Bristol BS99 7DX

Printed and bound in Great Britain by
William Clowes (Beccles) Limited,
Beccles and London

Foreword

In his foreword to the first edition in 1971, Peter Loose described liquidations as something of a growth industry. Experience since 1971 has shown that liquidations have remained a growth industry and that the complexities of administering a voluntary liquidation have been increased by a wealth of additional legislation and decided case-law. In these circumstances, although our original intention was simply to re-edit *Loose* it proved necessary to rewrite substantial parts of the book.

We are very grateful to Mr. Stephen Allcock for contributing Appendix 7 to this edition.

The law is attempted to be stated as at 1st January 1981.

MICHAEL CRYSTAL
JOHN HIGHAM

The Temple
London EC4

1st January 1981

Save where stated to the contrary, references in this book to sections are to the Companies Act 1948 as amended and those to rules are to the Companies (Winding-Up) Rules 1949 as amended.

Contents

Table of Cases

Table of Statutes

Companies Act 1948 (*cont.*)

Table of Statutory Instruments

CHAPTER 1

Check-List for a Voluntary Winding-Up

This Check-List has been placed at the front of the book in the hope that it may be convenient for reference. Cross-references are given to the page where each subject is discussed in detail, and where each form is set out.

The numbering of the forms can cause difficulty as some textbooks and printed forms use numbers, without indicating their source.

There are three possibilities: a form may bear the number allocated to it by:

(a) The Appendix to the Companies (Winding-Up) Rules 1949. (S.I. 1949. 330)
or (b) The Companies (Forms) Regulations 1979
or (c) The Publishers of the form.

Throughout this book, all forms, other than the author's specimens or precedents, are distinguished by (R) if they are in the Rules, (F) if in the Regulations and (J) if published by Jordan & Sons Limited.

1. Check-List for a Members' Winding-Up

Step to be taken	Page	Time Limit	Rule (R) Section (s)	Form	Page
1. *Declaration of Solvency* to be made incorporating statement of Assets and Liabilities	17	Within 5 weeks before Resolution	s.283	108 (R) W.U.R. 108 (J)	126
2. *Declaration to be Filed*	17	Before the date of the meeting	s.283	108 (R) W.U.R. 108 (J)	126

Step to be taken	Page	Time Limit	Rule (R) Section (s)	Form	Page
3. *Give Notice to Members of* Meeting to pass special Resolution and appoint Liquidator	17	21 days clear subject to waiver by 95%	s.278(1)(b) s.133(3)(b)	CA 71 (J)	128
4. *Members' Meeting.* When Resolution passed (75% majority) *Publish Notice in Gazette*	20	14 days from Resolution	s.279	CA 70A (J)	134
5. *File copy Resolution with Registrar*	20	15 days from Resolution	s.143	CA 70 (J)	135
6. *Publish Notice of Appointment of Liquidator in Gazette*	20	14 days from Resolution	s.305	39 E (F) 39 E (J)	138
7. *File Notice of Appointment of Liquidator with Registrar*	20	14 days from Resolution	s.305	39 C (F) 39 C (F)	139
8. *Statement of Liquidation* on all letters, invoices and orders	21	Immediately	s.338		
9. *Take into custody* seal, cheques, papers, books documents and property	28	Immediately	s.243		
10. *Letter to Creditors* to submit details of claims with formal *Notice to Claim*	42	14 days' notice	ss.316, 317 R.106	Specimen CA 74 (J)	141 142
11. *Advertise Notice to Claim* in *Gazette* and one *Local Newspaper*	43	14 days' notice	R.106	CA 74A (J)	143

Step to be taken	Page	Time Limit	Rule (R) Section (s)	Form	Page
12. *Letter to Creditors* who have claimed enclosing *Proof of Debt* for completion	44	None	R.94	59, 59A (R) W.U.R. 59A (J)	146 148
13. *Examine Proofs* and admit or reject	44	None	R.107	61 (R) W.U.R. 61 (J)	149
14. *Settle Priorities* and *validity* of Preferential, Secured and Unsecured Creditors where necessary	44, 82	None	s.319 R.95, 141		
15. *Settle List of Contributories* and make calls where necessary	87, 88	None	s.303(1)		
16. *File statement* and affidavit with Registrar, where winding-up continues for more than 1 year. Pay unclaimed moneys into Insolvency Services Account when held for 6 months	35 28	30 days from end of first 12 months	s.342 R.196–198 s.343 R.199	92–96 (R) W.U.R. 92–96	150–158
17. Where 16 applies *call general meeting* and lay accounts	35, 51	3 months from end of year on 14 days' notice	s.289	CA 98 (J)	159
18. *Half-yearly* after first year *file documents* as in 16 above	35	Immediately after end of each 6 month period	R.197, 198	92–96 (R) W.U.R. 92–96	150–158
19. *Yearly after* first year hold *general meeting* as in 17	35	As 17	s.289 R.129	CA 98 (J)	159

Step to be taken	Page	Time Limit	Rule (R) Section (s)	Form	Page
20. *Distribute assets in due order* i.e.	80–91		ss. 316, 317		
(a) Costs (including Remuneration) of Winding-Up			s.309		
(b) Preferential Debts			s.319(1)		
(c) Floating Charges			s.319(5)		
(d) Ordinary Debts			s. 302		
(e) Surplus to Members			s.302		
(f) Undistributed sums to Bank of England			s. 343 R.199		
21. *Prepare Final Account*	92		s.290(1)	110 (R) W.U.R. 110 (J)	162
22. *Notice to Members of Final Meeting,* including Extra-ordinary	92	1 month's notice	s.290	CA 75 (J)	164
Resolution to dispose of books and papers	93		s.341		
23. *Publish* Notice of Final Meeting in *Gazette*	92	1 month's notice	s.290	CA 75A (J)	165
24. *File Account and Return* of Final Meeting with Registrar (dissolution occurs 3 months later)	94	1 week from meeting	s.290	110 (R) W.U.R. 110, 111 (J)	161
25. *File Extraordinary Resolution to dispose* of books and papers, with Registrar	93	15 days from meeting	s.143	51A (J)	171

2. *Check-List for a Creditor's Winding-Up*

Step to be taken	Page	Time Limit	Rule (R) Section (s)	Form	Page
1. Directors prepare (a) *Statement of affairs* (b) *List of Creditors* and appoint chairman of Creditors' Meeting	19	Before Creditors' Meeting	s.293(3)	Specimen	129
2. Give *Notice to Members* of Meeting to (a) pass Extraordinary Resolution (b) appoint Liquidator and (c) appoint five nominees to Committee of Inspection	18	14 days' notice (7 if unlimited Company)	s.278(1)(c)	Specimen	130
3. Give *Notice to Creditors* of Meeting to be held on the same day or the day after the Members' Meeting.	18	Simultaneously with Members' Notice	s.293(1)	CA 76 (J)	131
Enclose General and Special *Proxies*			R.146–156	80, 81 (R) W.U.R. 80/81 (J)	132
4. *Advertise* Creditors' Meeting in *Gazette* and two *local newspapers*	18	Before meeting	s.293(2)	CA 76a (J)	133
5. Give Notice that meetings called, to Creditors and *Sheriffs* where *executions pending*	19	Simultaneously with Members' Notice	s.325 s.326 R.43	CA 76 (J)	131
6. Hold Members' Meeting and *pass Extraordinary Resolution* (75% majority). If not passed, the undermentioned steps cannot be taken	19	As specified in Notices	s.278(1)(c)		

Step to be taken	Page	Time Limit	Rule (R) Section (s)	Form	Page
7. At meetings Members appoint their nominees as *Liquidator* and *Members of Committee of Inspection*	58		s.294 s.295(1)		
8. *Hold Creditors' Meeting* to consider statement of affairs etc. and decide whether to accept Members' nominees for Liquidator and Committee of Inspection or to make different appointments. Resolutions require majority in Number and Value	21, 58	As specified in notices, i.e. day of Members' Meeting or following day	s.294 s.295		
9. *Publish Extra-ordinary Resolution in Gazette*	21	14 days from Resolution	s.279	CA 73A (J)	136
10. *File copy Extraordinary Resolution with Registrar*	21	15 days from Resolution	s.143	CA 73 (J)	137
11. *Publish Notice of Appointment of Liquidator in Gazette*	21	14 days from Resolution	s.305	39E (F) 39E (J)	138
12. *File Notice of Appointment of Liquidator with Registrar*	21	14 days from Resolution	s.305	39D (F) 39D (J)	140
13. *Statement of Liquidation* on all letters, invoices and orders	22	Immediately	s.338		

Step to be taken	Page	Time Limit	Rule (R) Section (s)	Form	Page
14. *Take into custody* seal, cheques, papers, books, documents and property	28	Immediately	s.243		
15. Call meetings of *Committee of Inspection* (if appointed)	58	At least once a month	s.253(2)		
16. *Call meetings of Creditors* when required, and enclose proxy forms	60	On 7 days' notice in Gazette, local paper and to every Creditor	R.127–129	75 (R)	179
17. *Letter to Creditors* to submit details of claims, with formal Notice to Claim	42	14 days' notice	s.316, 317 R.106	Specimen CA 74 (J)	141 142
18. Advertise *Notice to Claim* in *Gazette* and one *local paper*	43	14 days' notice	R.106	CA 74A (J)	143
19. *Letter to Creditors* who have claimed enclosing *Proof of Debt* for completion	44	None	R.94	59 (R) W.U.R. 59A (J) 59A (R)	146 148
20. *Examine Proofs* and admit or reject	44	None	R.107	61 (R) W.U.R. 61 (J)	149
21. *Settle Priorities and Validity* of Preferential, Secured and Unsecured Creditors	44, 82	None	s.319 R.95, 141		
22. *Settle List of Contributories* and make calls where necessary	87, 88	None	s.303(1)		

Step to be taken	Page	Time Limit	Rule (R) Section (s)	Form	Page
23. *File statement and Affidavit* with Registrar where Winding-Up continues for more than 1 year	35	30 days from end of first 12 months	s.342 R.196, 198	92–96 (R) W.U.R. 92–96 (J)	150–158
Pay unclaimed moneys into Bank of England	28	When held for 6 months	s.343 R.199		
24. Where 23 applies call *General Meeting* by Notice to *Members* and lay accounts before it	35	3 months from end of year on 14 days' notice	s.299	CA 98 (J)	159
25. Where 23 applies call *Creditors' meeting* and lay accounts before it. Give notice to each Creditor (with proxies) and *Publish* in *Gazette* and one *local paper*	35, 60–61	3 months from end of year on 7 days' notice	s.299 R.129 R.148	Specimen	160
26. *Half-yearly after first year file documents* as in 23 above	35	Immediately after end of each 6-month period	R.197, 198	92–96 (R) W.U.R. 92–96 (J)	150–158
27. Yearly after first year *hold meetings* as in 24 and 25 above	35, 60	As 24 and as 25 above	s.289 R.129	CA 98 (J) Specimen	159 160
28. *Distribute assets in due order* i.e.	80–91		ss. 316, 317		
(a) Costs (including Remuneration) of Winding-Up			s.309		
(b) Preferential debts			s.319(1)		
(c) Floating charges			s.319(5)		

Step to be taken	Page	Time Limit	Rule (R) Section (s)	Form	Page
28. (*Continued*)					
(d) Ordinary debts			s.302		
(e) Surplus to Members			s.302		
(f) Undistributed sums to Bank of England			s. 343 R.199		
29. *Prepare Final Accounts*	92		s.300(1) R.182	110 (R) W.U.R. 110 (J)	162
30. *Notice to Members of Final Meeting*	92	1 month's notice	s.300	CA 78 (J)	cf. 170
31. *Publish* Notice of Members' Final Meeting in *Gazette*	92	1 month's notice	s.300	CA 78A (J)	170
32. *Notice to Creditors* of *Final Meeting*	92	1 month's notice	s.300	CA 77 (J)	cf. 169
33. *Publish Notice* of Creditors' Final Meeting in *Gazette*	92	1 month's notice	s.300	CA 77A (J)	169
34. *File Account and Return* of Final Meetings with Registrar (dissolution occurs 3 months later)	94	1 week from meeting	s.300	110 (R) W.U.R. 110, 112 (J)	166
35. *Dispose of Books and Papers* in accordance with Resolution of *Committee of Inspection*	93	Time specified in Resolution or at end of 5 years from dissolution	s.341(1) s.341(2)		

CHAPTER 2

Status of a Liquidator

A prospective Liquidator should consider carefully before he agrees to act. His duties are onerous and quite likely to bring him into conflict with the very persons who have asked for his services. This can be the experience of any Liquidator who finds himself making claims against his former clients for moneys due to a company, or for breach of their duties as Directors.

The current Guide to Professional Ethics of the Institute of Chartered Accountants in England and Wales provides that where an accountant or any of his partners or employees of his practice has or during the previous two years has had a continuing professional relationship with a company, no partner or employee of the practice should accept appointment as Liquidator of the Company if the Company is insolvent. Where the Company is solvent the Institute recommends that such appointments should not be accepted without careful consideration being given to the implications of acceptance in the particular case concerned. Similarly where an accountant or any of his partners or employees of his practice is or during the previous two years has been receiver of any assets of the Company the Institute advises that no partner or employee of the practice should accept appointment as Liquidator.

This book is principally concerned with the role of a Liquidator in a *Voluntary Winding-Up*, i.e. a winding-up controlled by the members or creditors and instituted in accordance with s. 278 and not (except where they overlap) with his role in the other two forms of liquidation, a *Compulsory Winding-Up by the Court* (cf. s. 222) and a *Voluntary Winding-Up under the Supervision of the Court* (cf. s. 311).[1]

The following table indicates that Voluntary Liquidations make up about 75% of the current total of liquidations in England and Wales:

[1] This latter mode of procedure is in any event largely obsolete.

Liquidations begun in	*1977*	*1978*	*1979*
Compulsory	2,425	2,265	2,064
Voluntary Under Supervision	—	—	—
Creditors' Voluntary	3,406	2,821	2,473
Members' Voluntary	3,650	3,615	4,030
Total	9,481	8,701	8,567

The rarity of Supervision Orders is probably due to the fact that Creditors, members and the Liquidator himself now have an express right of access to the Court to settle questions arising in any Voluntary Winding-Up, just as in the case of a Supervision Order or a Compulsory Winding-Up (s. 307).

Before examining in detail the powers and duties of a voluntary liquidator it may assist to give some general consideration to the nature of such an office and to consider whether any classification thereof is possible. This at once illustrates some of the problems with which a Liquidator is liable to be confronted. The role of a Liquidator is partly that of a trustee, partly that of an agent and partly that of an officer of the company appointed for the purpose of winding up its affairs and terminating its existence. Nonetheless, a Liquidator is none of those things in the fullest sense of the words.

(1) *Liquidator as Trustee*

A Liquidator is often described as a trustee and he has duties to the Creditors and the contributories to administer the funds of the Company which are said to be impressed with a trust for these parties.[1] Thus he must not make a secret profit out of his office (Rules 159–162) and his obligation as Trustee for the Creditors prevents time from running under the Limitation Acts 1939 to 1980 after winding-up has commenced. There are several points of difference, however:

(a) The fiduciary obligations of a voluntary Liquidator are owed primarily to the Company and Creditors as a body and not to individual creditors. So, in *Leon* v *York-O-Matic Limited*[2] where a Liquidator was alleged to have sold certain launderettes the property of the Company of which he was appointed at an under value, Plowman J. held that prima facie the proper complainant was the Company itself. There are, however,

[1] *Re Black & Co.'s Case* (1872) 8 Ch. App. 254; *Re Oriental Inland Steam Co.* (1874) 9 Ch. App. 557.

[2] [1966] 1 W.L.R. 1456.

express powers for any contributory or Creditor to apply to the Court if aggrieved by any act of the Liquidator. These powers are given by ss. 245(3) and 246(5), in the case of a Compulsory Winding-Up, but s.307 applies the Court's powers in these cases to a Voluntary Winding-Up also.[1]

(b) The general remedy for a person injured by an act of the Liquidator is not an action for breach of trust but one for breach of statutory duty[2] or a misfeasance summons under s.333.

(c) Normally trust property vests in a trustee who is personally liable on contracts which he makes in such capacity. The Company's property does not, however, vest in the Liquidator (unless the Court orders otherwise under s.244 in the case of a Compulsory Winding-Up).[3] The Company continues in existence and the Liquidator enters into contracts and deals with its property on the Company's behalf. He does not, therefore, normally assume personal liability under his contracts.[4]

(d) Furthermore, where prior to the commencement of a liquidation a company holds property as constructive trustee a voluntary Liquidator does not himself become automatically subject to the duties of a constructive trustee.[5] Even where a Liquidator deals with the property in question he will still not become liable as a constructive trustee provided that he acts honestly and reasonably and without notice of the trusts affecting the property concerned.[6]

(e) A Liquidator is not, it would seem, entitled to the relief afforded to trustees by the *Trustee Act 1925* (ss.23, 30 and 61) cf. *Re Windsor Steam Coal Company (1901) Limited*[7] where it was held that a Liquidator who had honestly but mistakenly paid a claim against the Company was personally liable to

[1] For the Court having jurisdiction to entertain applications in a voluntary winding-up cf. ss.218 and 455(1) which provide inter alia in addition to the general jurisdiction of the High Court for the local jurisdiction of County Courts over Companies whose registered offices are situate within their district and whose paid up share capital does not exceed £120,000.

[2] *Pulsford* v *Devenish* [1903] 2 Ch. 625.

[3] Cf. *Ayerst* v *C. & K. (Construction) Limited* [1976] A.C. 167 per Lord Diplock at p.177E.

[4] *Stead Hazel & Company* v *Cooper* [1933] I.K.B. 840.

[5] *Competitive Insurance* v *Davies Investments Limited* [1975] 1 W.L.R. 1240.

[6] Ibid.

[7] [1928] 1 Ch. 690 per Maugham J. confirmed on other grounds in the Court of Appeal whose decision is reported at [1929] 1 Ch. 151.

repay it. It may be, however, that in view of the wider application of the provisions of s.448 so as to include "officers" of a company a Liquidator today would be able to claim the protection of the provisions of that section which are similar to the provisions of s.61 of the Trustee Act 1925 in providing for the relief of officers and auditors who have acted honestly and reasonably and ought fairly to be excused.

(f) Some further insight, however, into the attitude of the modern Liquidator can perhaps be obtained from the judgement of Brightman J. in *Re Southard & Co. Limited*[1] where the learned judge quoted from the affidavit of the joint Liquidators in that case which accepted the moral obligation of a voluntary Liquidator to carry out work in some cases even where little or no remuneration could be expected.

(2) *Liquidator as Agent*

(a) In many ways a Liquidator may be described as a cross between a trustee and an agent or, alternatively, like the directors, whose powers terminate upon the commencement of a winding-up, as a fiduciary agent of the Company. Thus a Liquidator must not only act bona fide and reasonably and exercise his powers for their proper purposes only but also is bound to exercise reasonable care and skill in the performance of his duties. Failure to exercise the necessary degree of skill and care may inter alia deprive him of his costs.[2]

(b) A Liquidator is also under a fiduciary duty in respect of the assets of the Company of which he is appointed and is debarred save by leave of the Court from either purchasing any part of such assets or alternatively from acquiring as Liquidator on behalf of the Company any goods for the carrying on of the business of the Company from any person whose connection with him is of such a nature as would result in his obtaining any portion of the profit, if any, arising out of the transaction, cf. Rules 161/162. Similarly, a Liquidator may be required to disgorge any secret profit made by him in consequence of or by virtue of his office as Liquidator.

(c) The Liquidator differs from the normal agent, however, in that he himself controls the actions of his principal, i.e. the Company. Furthermore his duties as agent of the Company

[1] [1979] 1 W.L.R. 546 at p.551; affirmed at [1979] 1 W.L.R. 1198.
[2] *Re Silver Valley Mines* (1882) 21 Ch. D. 381.

are subject to his over-riding statutory duties to apply the Company's assets in paying Creditors and to distribute any surplus amongst the members.[1]

(3) *Liquidator as an Officer of the Company*

(a) A Liquidator is not expressly included in the definition of "officer" in s.455, but it would seem that this definition is not exhaustive, providing as it does only that "officer" "*includes* a director, manager or secretary".
(b) A Liquidator is expressly within the ambit of s.333 (misfeasance summons) and proceedings may be taken against him under this section for misfeasance or breach of duty. These proceedings may be brought by any creditor or by any "contributory", i.e. past or present member.
(c) He is also an officer of the Company for the purpose of his duty to file certain documents arising in the course of winding-up, and the resolutions and agreements mentioned in s.143.[2]

In *Re The Home & Colonial Insurance Company Limited*[3] Maugham J. referred to the "high standard of care and diligence" required from a Liquidator and pointed to the only refuge on which he can rely with complete safety—namely the right "in every case of serious doubt or difficulty—to submit the matter to the Court and obtain its guidance".

Under s.307 a voluntary Liquidator is entitled to "apply to the Court to determine any question arising in the winding-up". This is a power which a Liquidator should not hesitate to use in cases of difficulty or where an error of judgement may have serious financial consequences. In *Re J. Russell Electronics Limited*[4] for instance a Liquidator who had mistakenly paid £200 to a solicitor for work done in connection with the Winding-Up meetings had to refund the money out of his own pocket.

Finally it should be noted that although a voluntary Liquidator is not an officer of the Court the rule in Ex parte James[5], which requires officers of the Court to behave honestly and fairly and to do the fullest equity, and in particular cases to refrain from taking full advantage of accrued legal rights where it would be unfair to do so,

[1] *Knowles* v *Scott* [1891] 1 Ch. 717.
[2] *Re X Company Limited* [1907] 2 Ch. 92.
[3] [1930] 1 Ch. 102, 125.
[4] [1968] 1 W.L.R. 1252.
[5] (1874) 9 Ch. App. 609.

does extend to a Liquidator in a compulsory winding-up[1] and, as a matter of principle therefore, it would appear that a voluntary Liquidator should observe the same high standards and, if in doubt, apply to the Court for directions.

[1] *Re Opera Limited* [1891] 2 Ch. 154; *Re Clifton Place Garage Limited* [1970] Ch. 477; *Re Wyvern Developments Limited* [1974] 1 W.L.R. 1097.

CHAPTER 3

Commencement of Winding-Up

In a compulsory Winding-Up a Liquidator is appointed by the Court and can, therefore, rely on the validity of his appointment. Before accepting office in a Voluntary Winding-Up, a prospective Liquidator must satisfy himself that it has been properly commenced. Failure by the Company to comply with the requirements of the Act can nullify his appointment, although in certain circumstances parties who by their conduct have acquiesced in the liquidation may be unable to take the point.[1] A Liquidator cannot, of course, be appointed without his consent.[2]

(1) *Types of Voluntary Winding-Up*

(a) *Members'*

A Voluntary Winding-Up must start in one of two ways. It will be a *Members' Voluntary Winding-Up* if (1) a majority of the directors (or both if there are only two) have made a statutory *Declaration of Solvency* to the effect that, in their opinion, the Company shall be able to pay its debts in full within (at most) twelve months (s.283(1)) *and* (2) the declaration has been made within the five weeks preceding the resolution to wind up and embodies a statement of the Company's assets and liabilities as at the latest practicable date before the making of the declaration (s.283(2)), *and* (3) the declaration is filed with the Registrar not later than the day before the resolution is passed.

(b) *Creditors'*

In all other circumstances the liquidation will be a *Creditors' Voluntary Winding-Up*. This is the inevitable result of omitting or defaulting in any one of the steps mentioned above and will ensue whether or not the members or Directors are aware of it (s.293).

[1] *Re Bailey Hay & Co. Ltd.* [1971] 1 W.L.R. 1357.

[2] *Re Highland and Northern Dairy Farms Limited* [1964] S.C. 1.

The steps which must be taken in each case and which the prospective Liquidator will wish to verify are as follows:

(2) *Preliminaries to Appointment of Liquidator in a Members' Voluntary Winding-Up*

(a) A *Declaration of Solvency* (Form 1 on p. 126) embodying a statement of assets and liabilities must have been made *within five weeks* before the date of the resolution to wind-up (s.283). However, accidental omissions or errors will not necessarily invalidate the statement so as to render it liable to be attacked under s.283(2)(b).[1]

(b) The Declaration of Solvency must have been *filed* before the date of the resolution (s.283).

(c) An Extraordinary General Meeting of members must have been summoned to pass a *special resolution* to wind-up (s.278(2)).

(d) *Twenty-one clear days' notice* (i.e. excluding the day of notice and the day of meeting) must have been given. The notice must specify the intention to propose a special resolution and set out either the entire text or the entire substance of the resolution[2] (s.141). (Form 2 on p. 128.)

(e) As an alternative to (1), a *majority in number* and 95% in nominal value of the voting members may *consent to short notice* (s.133(3)).

(f) A *quorum* must be present at the meeting.
   (i) The quorum may be fixed by the Articles (s.134).
   (ii) If the Company adopts *Table A. Article 53* the quorum will be three members present in person (i.e. not proxies).
   (iii) If Table A. Article 53 is excluded and the Articles are silent, the quorum will be two members personally present, s.134(e) as amended by the Companies Act 1980.

(g) The *special resolution* to wind-up must be passed by a *three-quarters majority* of the votes cast. However, it appears that a resolution for the Voluntary Winding-Up of a Company to which all the members have given their informal assent may be treated as having been validly passed notwithstanding the fact that no formal meeting of the members has taken place.[3]

[1] *de Courcy* v *Clement* [1971] Ch. 693.

[2] *Re Moorgate Mercantile Holdings Limited* [1980] 1 W.L.R. 227.

[3] *Re M. J. Shanley Contracting Ltd.* (1979) 124 Sol. J. 239 (following Re Duomatic Ltd. [1969] 2 Ch. 365).

(3) *Preliminaries to Appointment of Liquidator in a Creditors' Voluntary Winding-Up*

(a) Where no declaration of solvency can be made, a company will normally summon an extraordinary general meeting to pass an *Extraordinary Resolution* that it cannot by reason of its liabilities continue its business and that it is advisable to wind-up (s.278(1)(c)).
This is what normally happens in practice, but there is nothing to prevent the Company, if it wishes, from passing the usual Special Resolution to wind-up voluntarily without specifying any reasons, under s.278(1)(b). It will still be a Creditors' Winding-Up if no Declaration of Solvency has been filed.

(b) *Fourteen clear days' notice* of the Extraordinary General Meeting (or seven in the case of an unlimited company) must be given (s.133(1)(b)) where it is proposed to pass an extraordinary resolution. Where it is proposed to pass a Special Resolution 21 clear days' notice is required under s.141(2). In each case the notice must specify the intention to propose the resolution and set out the entire text or the entire substance of the resolution.[1] Alternatively the short notice provisions of s.133 may in the appropriate circumstances be invoked, see Re Centrebind Limited.[2]

(c) From the point of view of the Company it is desirable for the Directors to include in the agenda of the meeting *Ordinary Resolutions appointing a Liquidator* of their choice (s.294) and up to *five members* of any *Committee of Inspection* which may be set up by the Creditors (s.295(1)).

(d) The Company must call a *meeting of Creditors* for the day of the Extraordinary General Meeting, or the next day, and notice to the Creditors must be sent out simultaneously with the notice to members (s.293(1)). The notice must include general and special proxy forms (Rules 146–156).
Notice to *members* can be as short as they desire if consent to short notice is given under s.133(3)(b), but the Creditors are required to be given at least fourteen days' notice. Failure to give such notice to the Creditors will not however render the appointment of a Liquidator by the members invalid, but at any subsequent meeting the Creditors may appoint a Liquidator of their choice.[3]

[1] *Re Moorgate Mercantile Holdings Ltd.* (ante).
[2] [1967] 1 W.L.R. 377.
[3] *Re Centrebind Ltd.* (*supra*).

(e) The Creditors' meeting must be *advertised*, once in the *Gazette* and once at least in two local *newspapers* (s.293(2)).

(f) The Directors must prepare and lay before the Creditors' meeting a *statement of affairs* and list of Creditors and must appoint one of themselves to preside at that meeting s.293(3). (Specimen statement of affairs on p. 129.)

(g) If any *executions* against the Company are uncompleted, notice of the meeting should be given at once to the Creditor concerned (s.325) and to the Sheriff (s.326). The Creditor will then be obliged to account to the Liquidator unless he has already recovered his debt (s.325(1)), and the Sheriff, who must hold the sums recovered by him for fourteen days, must do the same, if the fourteen days period has not expired (s.326(2)).
Sections 325 and 326 refer to notice of the *Members'* meeting, but it has been held to be sufficient if the Sheriff gets notice of the *Creditors'* meeting.[1]

(h) There must be a *quorum* at the Members' meeting and the extraordinary resolution to wind-up must be passed by a *majority of three-quarters* of the votes cast. Failing this, the voluntary liquidation will be invalid[2] unless all the members can be taken to have given their informal consent to the passing of the resolution to wind-up the Company.[3]

Acceptance of Appointment

The prospective Liquidator must satisfy himself that the above steps have been properly taken. If not, he should refuse to accept his appointment. If, for example, he seriously doubts whether a company will be able to pay its debts within the period specified in the Declaration of Solvency, he should decline to act, and should advise the Directors to call an immediate meeting of Creditors so that their wishes as to the choice of Liquidator can be ascertained.

Under section 288 if at any time a Liquidator in a Members' Winding-Up considers that the debts will not be paid within the stated period, he is required to summon forthwith a meeting of Creditors and to lay before it a statement of the assets and liabilities of the Company.

A further precaution which a Liquidator should take is to make a Company search. In one case a Liquidator proceeded with his

[1] *Engineering Industry Training Board* v. *Samuel Talbot (Engineers) Limited* [1969] 2 Q.B. 270.

[2] But see *Re Bailey Hay & Co. Ltd.* (*ante*).

[3] *Re M. J. Shanley Contracting Ltd.* (1979) 124 Sol. J. 239.

administration but found when he was about to distribute assets that the Company had been struck off the Register under s.353 before the commencement of the liquidation. The Liquidator had then to apply to the Court by way of originating summons for a declaration under s.352(1) that the dissolution was void. Megarry J. held that although he could not be Liquidator of a Company which did not exist, he had sufficient standing, as a "person who appears to the Court to be interested", to entitle him to apply for the declaration, which would put him back into control.[1]

If, however, the Liquidator is satisfied with the preliminary steps he can take office, for which the procedure is as follows:

(4) *Procedure on Appointment of Liquidator in a Members' Winding-Up*

(a) The power (and indeed the duty) to appoint a Liquidator is vested in the Company in general meeting by s.285(1).

(b) The appointment is usually made at the meeting at which the resolution for Voluntary Winding-Up is passed. However, the appointment can be made at any meeting and only an ordinary resolution (i.e. a simple majority) is required. Notice of intention to make the appointment need not be given. Thus in *Re Trench Tubeless Tyre Company*[2] a Liquidator other than the one specified in the notice was elected. The appointment was held to be valid as there was no requirement to give notice that another candidate was to be appointed.

(c) One member alone cannot validly constitute a general meeting for the purpose of appointing a Liquidator. *In Re London Flats Limited*[3] the only other member left the room before the resolution was put and it was held that, from that moment, there was no meeting and therefore a Liquidator could not be appointed.

(d) If, for any cause whatever, there is no Liquidator acting, the Court can appoint one (s.304(1)), or replace an existing Liquidator (s.304(2)). A Corporation cannot act as Liquidator (s.335).

(e) A copy of the resolution to wind-up (which need not be printed, C.A. 1967, s.51) must be filed with the Registrar within fifteen days after the meeting (s.143) and advertised in

[1] *Re Wood & Martin (Bricklaying Contractors) Limited* [1971] 1 W.L.R. 293.
[2] [1900] 1 Ch. 408.
[3] [1969] 1 W.L.R. 711.

the *Gazette* within fourteen days (s.279). (See Forms 7 and 8 on pp. 134, 135).

(f) The Liquidator must, within fourteen days of his appointment, file a notice of appointment with the Registrar (Form 39C) and publish it in the *Gazette* (Form 39E) (s.305). (See Forms 11 and 12 on pp. 138, 139).

(g) A statement that the Company is being wound-up, e.g. "A.B.C. Limited (in Voluntary Liquidation)", must be made on every letter-heading, invoice or order (s.338).

(5) *Procedure on Appointment of Liquidator in a Creditors' Winding-Up*

(a) The power to appoint is vested in the Company in general meeting and its Creditors (s.294).

(b) The members may at the Winding-Up meeting, nominate a Liquidator, and if no other person is nominated by the Creditors, he will act (s.294).

(c) At their meeting, which will have been called pursuant to s.293, the Creditors will consider whether or not to accept the members' nominee, if any. If they reject him they may appoint their own nominee who will then become Liquidator (s.294).

(d) If the members' nominee is rejected by the Creditors any director, member or creditor may within seven days of the date of the Creditors' nomination apply to the Court *inter alia* for an order appointing the members' nominee, either solely or jointly with the Creditors' nominee, or alternatively appointing some other person to be Liquidator (s.294).

(e) The members' appointment will be by way of ordinary resolution (simple majority in voting rights), but the Creditors' appointment must be by resolution carried in accordance with Rule 134. This requires a majority in number and value of the Creditors present personally or by proxy and in *Re Caston Cushioning Limited*[1] a nomination by a majority in value only was held invalid.

(f) A prospective Liquidator must not, except by the direction of a meeting of Creditors or contributaries, use any solicitation in obtaining proxies or in procuring his appointment as Liquidator (Rule 151). If a Liquidator fails to observe this rule the Court may disallow his remuneration. Furthermore, a prospective Liquidator must not use any proxies held by him

[1] [1955] 1 W.L.R. 163.

to vote in favour of a resolution for the appointment of either himself or any partner or employer of his as Liquidator (Rule 153).

(g) The other steps are similar to those in a Members' Winding-Up, i.e. the resolution and the notice of appointment must be filed and published and the words "in Voluntary Liquidation" added to the Company's name on every letter-heading, invoice or order.[1]

[1] As to the appointment of a committee of inspection see pp. Ch. 8, *post*.

CHAPTER 4

Effects of Winding-Up and of the Appointment of Liquidator

As these two events frequently occur in quick succession it is convenient to consider their effects at the same time.

Date of Commencement

The date of the commencement of a Voluntary Winding-Up is the date of passing the resolution: s.280. (In the case of a Compulsory Winding-Up the commencement dates back to the presentation of the petition: s.229.)

From the date of commencement of a Voluntary Liquidation the effects are as follows:

(1) *Business Ceases*

The Company must cease to carry on business, except as required for the purpose of winding-up: s.281. However, the Liquidator has power on his own authority under s.303(1)(b) to continue the business for the beneficial winding-up of the Company.

(2) *Powers of Company*

The Company and its powers continue in existence until the Company is dissolved: s.281.

(3) *Company's Property*

The Company's property remains vested in it and does not pass to the Liquidator. Under s.244 in a Compulsory Winding-Up the Court can order the property of a company to vest in the Liquidator and this power can also be exercised by the Court in a Voluntary Winding-Up on application under s.307.

(4) *Share Transfers*

Transfers of shares, without the Liquidator's consent, and alterations in the status of members are void: s.282. However, the Liquidator may give such consent without referring to the Court and can make the appropriate entries in the Register of Members.[1] The transfer of debentures is not affected.[2]

(5) *Proceedings may be restrained*

Proceedings against the Company are not automatically stayed, as they are in a Compulsory Winding-Up (s.231), but the Court may restrain such proceedings on an application by a Liquidator, member or Creditor under s.307.[3] This power to restrain proceedings is likely to be exercised where a litigant against a company in voluntary liquidation seeks to upset the requirements of s.302 under which all non-preferential Creditors should rank *pari passu*. Some guidance as to whether the Court will stay proceedings in a Voluntary Winding-Up may be found in such cases as *Eastern Holdings Establishment of Vaduz* v *Singer & Friedlander Limited*,[4] (interpleader summons stayed) and *Langley Construction (Brixham) Limited* v *Wells*[5] (counterclaim against Company for amount in excess of Company's claim) (both compulsory liquidation cases).

(6) *Directors' Powers Cease*

In a Members' Winding-Up, the Directors' powers cease on the appointment of the Liquidator except in so far as the Company, or the Liquidator, allows them to continue, s.285(2), (e.g. in *Re Salisbury Railway Company*[6] the Liquidator allowed the Directors to exercise their powers so as to supervise the functioning of the Company's corn market).

In a Creditors' Winding-Up, the Directors' powers similarly cease except in so far as the Committee of Inspection, or (if there is no Committee) the Creditors, allow them to continue (s.296(2)).

[1] *Re National Bank of Wales* [1897] 1 Ch. 298.
[2] *Re Goy and Company Limited* [1900] 2 Ch. 149.
[3] *Westbury* v *Twigg Company Limited* [1892] 1 Q.B. 77.
[4] [1967] 1 W.L.R. 1017.
[5] [1969] 1 W.L.R. 503.
[6] [1969] 1 Ch. 349.

(7) *Employees*

A Voluntary Winding-Up does not necessarily terminate the service contracts of employees other than Directors,[1] but the winding-up, combined with the surrounding circumstances, such as the cessation of the Company's business, may have this effect, e.g. by amounting to a repudiation of a seven-year agency agreement.[2]

(8) *Rights of Inspection*

Rights of members and others to inspect the Company's registers of members and charges cease[3] but they can apply to the Court for an inspection (ss.266 and 307).

(9) *Floating Charges*

Floating charges crystallise[4] and, if made within the preceding twelve months, are invalid except as to the amount of any cash paid at the time of or subsequently to the creation of and in consideration for the charge, unless the Company was solvent immediately after the creation of the charge (s.322).[5]

(10) *Effect on Certain Assets*

Many leases and certain other commercial agreements will become liable to forfeiture, but this depends on the terms of the agreement in each case. They are not necessarily automatically terminated by the winding-up. The Liquidator himself has certain powers to disclaim under s.323 (see under "Powers of Liquidator", pp. 39–41, *post*).

(11) *Control of Assets*

Control of the Company's affairs and custody of all its property passes to the Liquidator, s.243(1).

[1] *Gerard* v *Worth of Paris Limited* [1936] 2 All E.R. 905; *Midland Counties District Bank* v *Attwood* [1905] 1 Ch. 357.

[2] *Reigate* v *Union Manufacturing Company* [1918] 1 K.B. 592; cf. *Fowler* v *Commercial Timber Co.* [1930] 2 K.B. 1.

[3] *Re Kent Coalfields Syndicate* [1898] 1 Q.B. 754.

[4] *Re Crompton & Company Limited* [1914] 1 Ch. 954.

[5] See pp. 49–50, *post*.

(12) *Executions and Attachments*

The Liquidator is under a duty, so far as possible, to recover the benefit of any executions or attachments issued against the Company. His rights in this respect are as follows:

(a) Where a Creditor has issued execution against the goods or lands of a company or has attached any debt due to the Company, he is not entitled to retain the benefit of the execution against the Liquidator unless he has completed the execution or attachment before the passing of the resolution for Voluntary Winding-Up (s.325(1)).

(b) However, where any creditor receives notice of the calling of a meeting to propose a resolution for Voluntary Winding-Up, he is not entitled to retain the benefit of any execution or attachment uncompleted at that date (s.325(1) proviso (a)).

(c) An execution against goods is completed by seizure and sale or by the making of a Charging Order under s.1 of the Charging Orders Act 1979 and an attachment of a debt is completed by the receipt of the debt, (s.325(2)).[1] An execution against land is completed by seizure, by the appointment of a receiver or by the making of a Charging Order under the Charging Orders Act 1979: (s.325(2)).[1]

(d) The rights conferred on the Liquidator under s.325(1) may nevertheless be set aside by the Court in its discretion, (s.325(1), proviso (c)). However, exceptional circumstances are required in a Creditors' Voluntary Winding-Up before the Court will set aside the Liquidator's rights[2] and thereby interfere with the general principal of *pari passu* distribution of a company's property amongst its unsecured Creditors.

(e) Where goods of a company are taken in execution and, before sale thereof or the completion of the execution by receipt and recovery of the full amount of the levy, notice is served on the sheriff that a resolution for Voluntary Winding-Up has been passed, the sheriff on request must deliver the goods and any money seized or received in part satisfaction of the execution to the Liquidator but the costs of the execution are a first charge on any such goods or money (s.326(1)).

(f) Where under an execution in respect of a judgement exceeding £250 goods of a company are sold or money is paid in order to avoid a sale, the sheriff is required to deduct the costs of the execution and to retain the balance for fourteen days. If

[1] As amended by s. 4 of the Charging Orders Act 1979.

[2] *Re Carribbean Products (Yam Importers) Ltd* [1966] Ch. 331.

within that time notice is served on him of the calling of a meeting to propose a resolution for Voluntary Winding-Up and the resolution is passed the sheriff must pay the balance to the liquidator (s.326(2)). If no such notice is served within the fourteen-day period the Creditor is entitled to the balance.[1]

(g) The rights conferred on a Liquidator under section 326 (1) and (2) can also be set aside by the Court in its discretion (s.326(3)). However, as under (d) above, exceptional circumstances will be required before the Court will do so.

[1] Cf. *Marley Tile Co. Ltd* v *Burrows* [1978] Q.B. 241.

CHAPTER 5

Duties of the Liquidator

The Liquidator's principal responsibilities are as follows:

(1) *Preliminary Duties*

Within fourteen days of his appointment the Liquidator must *publish notice* of his appointment in the *Gazette* and *file it* with the Registrar (s.305). He should ensure that the Winding-Up resolution is duly filed (*within fifteen days: s.143*) and published in the *Gazette* (*within fourteen days: s.279*). He must have the Company described as "in Liquidation" on all letter-headings, invoices and orders (s.338).

(2) *Duty to Take Possession of Property*

The Company's property does not vest in the Liquidator, but he is under a duty to take all the Company's property into his custody: s.243.

(3) *Duty as to Bank Accounts*

(a) In a Voluntary Winding-Up a Liquidator must pay any moneys representing unclaimed or undistributed assets which have remained in his hands for more than six months into the Insolvency Services Account at the Bank of England (s.343). The duty of a Liquidator under the section to pay into the Insolvency Services Account any money held by a company in respect of dividends or other sums due to any person as a member of the company does not however extend to moneys held to pay debts owed to members who cannot be traced and whose claims have been excluded by virtue of the application of Rule 106.[1] Assets which are required for a specific purpose, e.g. a s.206 Scheme, are not "undistributed".[2]

[1] *Re Compania de Electricidad de la Provincia de Buenos Aires Ltd.* [1980] Ch. 146. For rule 106 see pp. 43–44, post.

[2] *Re Land Mortgage Bank of Florida* [1898] 1 Ch. 444.

(b) In a Creditors' Voluntary Winding-Up, if the Committee of Inspection, or, if there is no Committee of Inspection, the Liquidator considers that there are surplus funds which should be invested, a certificate should be signed and transmitted to the Department of Trade with a request that the Department make the investments required (Rule 173).

(c) Balances in excess of £2,000 in the Insolvency Services Account at the Bank of England earn interest at 2% only or at the rate fixed by Treasury Order. At present that rate is 3½%.[1]

(d) The Liquidator can continue to use the Company's existing banking facilities, either in the name of the Company "In Liquidation" or in his own name. He should take over all cheque books and send to the bank a copy of the resolution appointing him, with instructions to stop all cheques which are still unpaid.

(4) *Duty to Settle List of Contributories*

The term "contributory" is defined in section 213 as meaning every person liable to contribute to the assets in a Winding-Up, including an alleged contributory. This includes *a holder of fully paid shares* since every member is under a primary liability to contribute, qualified only by the provisions of s.212(1)(d) that a member's liability shall not be greater than the amount unpaid on his shares. However, where a Company has carried on business for more than six months with fewer than two members any person who, for the whole or any part of the period it so carries on business after those six months, is a member of the Company and knows that it is carrying on business with only one member is jointly and severally liable with the Company for payment of the whole of the debts of the Company contracted during that period (s.31).[2]

The Liquidator has the power, which in a compulsory liquidation is exercised by the Court, to settle a List of Contributories and to make calls (s.303(1)(c) and (d)). The list is prima facie evidence of the liability of the persons named therein to be contributories (s.303(1)(c)).

In practice the Liquidator will only rarely need to make calls, as unpaid and partly paid up shares are not common. Where the Liquidator settles a List of Contributories for the purpose of making

[1] See The Companies Liquidation Account (Interest) Order 1965 (S.I. 1965 No. 920).

[2] As amended by the Companies Act 1980.

calls he can adopt his own procedure, but in so doing should have regard to the procedure applicable in a compulsory liquidation (see Rules 80–85).

Where there is a surplus for members in the liquidation, the Liquidator will need to verify the Register of Members and on making a distribution, according to the rights of the members under s.302, to take up the share certificates as appropriate.

(5) *Duty to Examine Conduct of Officers*

(a) The Liquidator has a duty to investigate the conduct of the Company's officers and to consider whether the Company's officers have been guilty of any wrongful conduct towards the Company. By virtue of sections 268 and 307 a Liquidator in a Voluntary Winding-Up may apply to the Court for an order for the examination of any Officer of the Company or person known or suspected to have in his possession any property of the Company or supposed to be indebted to the Company or any person whom the Court deems capable of giving information concerning the promotion, formation, trade, dealings, affairs or property of the Company.

(b) The Court has a discretion whether to order an examination but will usually do so where the examination is required for the benefit of the winding-up and the Liquidator has not already decided to commence legal proceedings against the proposed examinee.[1] Save in very exceptional circumstances the examination will be held in private.[2] The Court also has power under sections 270 and 307 to order the public examination of a director but such an order is rarely obtained.

(c) The right to apply for an order under section 268 is an extremely valuable power in the hands of the Liquidator which he should not hesitate to use where appropriate. However, the Liquidator must be careful not to use the power oppressively and in many cases the Court will require the Liquidator to make written enquiries, e.g. by questionnaire, before making an order.[3] A Creditor or a contributory may also apply under section 307 for an order under section 268 but such an application may be treated with caution by the Court.

[1] *Re Castle New Homes Ltd* [1979] 1 W.L.R. 1075; *Re Spiraflite* [1979] 1 W.L.R. 1096.

[2] *Re Property Insurance Co.* [1914] 1 Ch. 775.

[3] *Re Rolls Razor* (No. 2) [1970] Ch. 576.

(6) *Duty to Recover Assets and to Institute Proceedings*

(a) If the Liquidator finds on his investigation of the accounts and records of the Company that the Directors have made a profit (apart from remuneration) out of their position[1] or if they have used the Company's money for their own personal benefit or drawn remuneration to which they are not entitled the Liquidator must require them to account for it.

(b) Recovery of Property and Money: s.258. Under sections 258 and 307 the Court may at any time after the passing of a resolution for Voluntary Winding-Up require any contributory, trustee, receiver, banker, agent or officer of the Company to pay, deliver, convey, surrender or transfer forthwith or as the Court may direct to the Liquidator any money, property or books and papers to which the Liquidator is prima facie entitled.

(c) Misfeasance Summons: s.333.

(i) Where in a Winding-Up the Court is satisfied that any past or present Director, Manager, Liquidator or Officer of a Company has misapplied or retained or become liable or accountable for any money or property of the Company or been guilty of any misfeasance or breach of trust in relation to the Company the Court on the application of the Liquidator or of any Creditor or contributory may compel repayment or restoration of the money or property of the Company with interest or require the payment of compensation to be made to the Company (s.333). Application under s.333 is made by way of summons and is an alternative to proceeding by way of action.

(ii) The section, which is procedural only, is directed at misfeasance and it is not intended to deal with acts or defaults which are merely negligent.[2] If the Liquidator wishes to complain of negligence he should proceed by action. Furthermore, a debenture holder's receiver and manager is not an officer for the purposes of this section.[3]

(d) *Fraudulent Trading: s.332.* If the Liquidator considers that any business of the Company has been carried on with *intent to defraud Creditors* or for any fraudulent purpose, he may apply to the Court for a declaration that those knowingly

[1] See eg *Regal (Hastings) Ltd.* v *Gulliver* [1942] 2 All E.R. 378.
[2] *Re B. Johnson & Co. (Builders) Ltd.* [1955] Ch. 634.
[3] *Ibid.*

party thereto shall be personally liable for all such debts of the Company as the Court may direct (s.332).

There must be actual dishonesty,[1] but fraudulent trading will usually be inferred if the Directors carry on business when they know that there is no reasonable prospect of the debts being paid.[2] A single transaction can amount to fraudulent trading,[3] but the giving of a fraudulent preference (see post) in itself will not.[4]

Where the Liquidator applies under s.332, the amount awarded to the Liquidator will form part of the general assets of the Company. However, in addition to the Liquidator a Creditor personally can apply under s.332 and the Court has power to order payment to him for his own benefit.[5] The Court will generally require the Creditor to notify the Liquidator of any such proceedings.[6]

The offending parties are also liable to criminal penalties (seven years' imprisonment and/or a fine or both) (s.332(3))[7] and can be barred from directorships or company management for up to five years (s.188).

(7) *Duty to Recover Fraudulent Preferences*

Any disposition of the Company's property, payment, or other transaction in favour of a Creditor, will be void against the Liquidator if it is a fraudulent preference effected within the six months preceding the commencement of the winding-up (s.320).

Section 320 incorporates the law of fraudulent preference for the time being in bankruptcy (currently s.44 Bankruptcy Act 1914). The salient features are as follows:

(i) The Company must have been insolvent at the time of the transaction.

(ii) The transaction must be with a view to giving the Creditor, or any surety or guarantor for the debt due to such Creditor, a preference over other Creditors.

[1] *Re Patrick & Lyon Limited* [1933] 1 Ch. 786.
[2] *Re Wm. C. Leitch Bros. Limited* [1932] 2 Ch. 71.
[3] *Re Gerald Cooper Chemicals Ltd.* [1978] Ch. 262.
[4] *Re Sarflax Ltd.* [1979] Ch. 592.
[5] *Re Cyona Distributors Ltd.* [1967] Ch. 889.
[6] *Re Gerald Cooper Chemicals Ltd. (ante).*
[7] As amended by the Companies Act 1980.

(iii) The essential requirement for a fraudulent preference is that the dominant intention of the Company was to prefer the Creditor.[1]

(iv) There need not be fraud in the moral sense, or indeed any moral blame at all.[2]

(v) An intention to prefer is necessary; there will be no fraudulent preference if a payment is made under real pressure, e.g. a threat of proceedings made against a Company which is seeking to avoid liquidation.

(vi) If a transaction is set aside under s.320 as a fraudulent preference of a person whose property is charged to secure the Company's debt, that person is put into the same position as if he were a surety for the debt to the extent of the charge or the value of his interest in the property charged, e.g. where a Director has deposited the deeds of his own property with a Bank to secure the Company's overdraft (s.321).

(vii) A promise to execute a charge on request may be regarded as a promise to prefer on request and hence as a fraudulent preference,[3] but the creation of a charge in pursuance of a pre-existing obligation (e.g. under a memorandum of deposit of title deeds securing a bank overdraft) will not, of itself, be a fraudulent preference.[4]

(viii) Where the dominant intention is not to prefer but for example to keep open a line of credit with a Bank in the interests of the Company payments made to the Bank will not amount to a fraudulent preference.[5]

(ix) Any sums recovered by the Liquidator are available for all the Creditors and do not become subject to a floating charge.[6]

A conveyance or assignment by a Company of all its property to trustees for the benefit of all its Creditors is also void (s.320(2)). It has been held therefore that under this subsection a floating charge created for the benefit of all the Creditors of a Company may be avoided.[7]

[1] *Sharpe* v *Jackson* [1899] A.C. 419; *Re Kushler (M) Limited* [1943] Ch. 248; *Re Cutts* [1956] 1 W.L.R. 728.

[2] *Re Patrick & Lyon Ltd.* [1933] 1 Ch. 786.

[3] *Re Eric Holmes (Property) Limited* [1965] Ch. 1052.

[4] *Re William Hall (Contractors) Limited* [1967] 1 W.L.R. 948.

[5] *Re FLE Holdings Limited* [1967] 1 W.L.R. 1409.

[6] *Re Yagerphone Limited* [1935] Ch. 392.

[7] *Re London Joint Bank* v *Herbert Dickinson* [1922] W.N. 13.

(8) *Duty to Pay Creditors*

It is the Liquidator's duty to ascertain and fix the liabilities of the Company, to advertise for Creditors, to admit or reject claims of Creditors, and to pay them, after payment of the expenses of Winding-Up: s.302.

In *Pulsford* v *Devenish*[1] the Liquidator omitted to pay one of the Creditors and allowed the Company to be dissolved. The Court held that the Liquidator was under a statutory duty to pay Creditors and as he had broken that duty he was personally liable. In *Re R–R Realisations Limited*[2] the Court reviewed the circumstances in which a Voluntary Liquidator can obtain an order for leave to distribute the assets of a Company amongst its members notwithstanding a last minute claim by persons claiming to be Creditors and held that the test to be applied in such cases was whether it was just to make such an order.

(9) *Duty to Distribute the Surplus*

After payment of all debts and other claims, any surplus must be distributed in accordance with the rights of the members: s.302. Any sums unclaimed or undistributed for six months after receipt must be paid into the Insolvency Services Account at the Bank of England and any person claiming to be entitled to any such moneys may apply to the Department of Trade for payment thereof: s.343.

If there is a dispute as to title to any moneys paid into the Insolvency Services Account the Court has jurisdiction to resolve the dispute.[3]

(10) *Duty to keep Accounts, Books and Papers*

A Liquidator cannot properly perform his duties without maintaining proper accounts. Furthermore, a Liquidator is placed under the following express statutory duties:

(a) If the Winding-Up is completed within a year, the Liquidator must make up a final account for the final meetings of members and Creditors (ss.290 and 300).

[1] [1903] 2 Ch. 625.
[2] [1980] 1 W.L.R. 805.
[3] *Birchin Lane Nominees Limited* v *Nicholson* [1969] 1 W.L.R. 1362.

(b) If the Winding-Up is not completed within a year of its commencement, at the end of that year and of each succeeding year, he must summon a general meeting of the Company and (in a Creditors' Winding-Up) of the Creditors and lay interim accounts before them (ss.289 and 299).

(c) Within thirty days after the end of the first year, and thereafter at half-yearly intervals, the Liquidator must render a statement in the prescribed form as appropriate (s.342 and Rules 197 and 198). (See Forms 18, 19, 20 at pp. 150–158.)

(d) Any Liquidator (whether the Liquidation is concluded or not) must render accounts and information to the Department of Trade at any time if so required (Rules 200–201).

(e) In a Creditors' Winding-Up, the Liquidator must keep such books as the Committee or (if none) the Creditors may direct (Rule 172(3)).

(f) Under s.341(1)(b) on dissolution the books and papers may be disposed of as directed by—
   (i) An extra-ordinary Resolution in a Members' Winding-Up;
   (ii) the Committee of Inspection or (if none) the Creditors in a Creditor's Winding-Up.

   The Liquidator's responsibility for his and the Company's books and papers terminates after five years from dissolution (s.341(2)).

(11) *Duty to Dissolve the Company*

When the Liquidator has completed his administration and, where appropriate, distributed any surplus assets he must call "*final meetings*" of the Members and (in a Creditor's Winding-Up) of the Creditors, and lay before them his final accounts for their approval. The meetings must be advertised one month beforehand in the *Gazette*.

Within one week of the meeting(s), the Liquidator must send a copy of the accounts and make a return to the Registrar of Companies of the holding of the meeting(s) and the date(s) thereof, Forms 23 and 26 on pp. 161, 166.

On receipt of the accounts and the return the Registrar will register them. On the expiration of three months from registration the Company is deemed to be dissolved unless in the interim any interested party obtains an order from the Court for the deferment of the date of dissolution. (See generally s.290 (members) and s.300 (creditors)).

CHAPTER 6

Powers of a Liquidator

The Liquidator's powers fall into the following categories.

(1) Section 303(1)(b) entitles him, on his own authority and without sanction, to exercise all the powers given to a Liquidator in a Compulsory Winding-Up, with three exceptions which are noted under (2) below.
The powers given to a Liquidator in a Compulsory Winding-Up by s. 245(1), and omitting the three exceptional cases, are:

(a) *To bring or defend actions* in the name of the Company (s. 245(1)(a)). If the Liquidator acts in the name of the Company, he is not personally liable for costs but *aliter* where he acts as Liquidator and institutes the proceedings in his own name.[1] He will, in any case, be entitled to an indemnity out of the assets unless he has acted improperly.[2]

(b) *To carry on the business* of the Company so far as necessary for beneficial Winding-Up (s.245(1)(b)). The Liquidator must exercise this power with care and with expert advice where necessary. It is not sufficient that the carrying on of the business will be of benefit to the Company—it must assist the beneficial Winding-Up[3]. The Liquidator will be justified in carrying on the business if he reasonably and bona fide believes that this will be the case, even if he is subsequently shown to have been mistaken.[4]
The debts properly incurred in carrying on the business rank prior to debts provable in the liquidation of the Company.[5]

(c) *To appoint a solicitor* to assist him in his duties (s. 245(1)(c)).[6]

[1] *Van Den Hurk* v *Martens & Company Limited* [1920] 1 K.B. 850.

[2] *Re Silver Valley Mines* (1882) 21 Ch. 381; Re *Wilson Lovatt & Sons Ltd.* [1977] 1 All E.R. 274.

[3] *Re Wreck Recovery Company* (1880) 15 Ch. D. 353.

[4] *Re Great Eastern Electric Company Limited* [1941] Ch. 241.

[5] *Re Davis (S) & Company* [1945] Ch. 402.

[6] In the case of a compulsory liquidation a Liquidator should be astute to ensure that proper sanction has been obtained although the Court has power to give a retrospective sanction cf, *Re Associated Travel Leisure Services Limited* [1978] 1 W.L.R. 547.

If there is a possibility of conflict of interest, the Court may set the appointment aside.[1]

(d) *To sell and transfer* the property of the Company (s. 245(2)(a)). This is one of the Liquidator's main tasks and may be carried out by public auction, or by private treaty. Agents may be appointed and paid (s.245(2)(g)). In a sale by auction, a reserve should be fixed, but the Court will not interfere unless the Liquidator is acting in a manner in which no reasonable Liquidator would act. Thus in *Leon* v *York-O-Matic Limited*[2] the Liquidator of a launderette company was in the course of selling seven launderettes to the husband of a former Director for £47,000. The plaintiff (also a former Director) offered £40,000 for only four of the launderettes and applied for an interlocutory injunction to stop the Liquidator's proposed sale, alleging that it was a sale at an undervalue. Plowman J. held that the Court should not interfere as there was no fraud, no evidence that the sale must be at an undervalue, or that this was a transaction which no reasonable Liquidator would enter into.

A Liquidator should not normally exchange the Company's property for shares in another company except under the procedure prescribed by s.287. A Liquidator must not buy the Company's seal, he will be personally liable if he enters into an agreement under seal in his own name.[3]

(e) *To act in the name of the Company* and to *execute and sign* any documents which may be necessary (s.245(2)(b)). In any transfer the Company is the transferring party since its property remains vested in it, but its seal is affixed and attested by the Liquidator, and he may be asked to join in a transfer to confirm it. In view of the Liquidator's power to use the Company's seal, he will be personally liable if he enters into an agreement under seal in his own name.[2]

(f) *To prove* in the Bankruptcy or insolvency of any contributory: s.245(2)(c).

(g) To draw, accept, make and indorse *bills of exchange* and promissory notes in the name of the Company: s. 245(2)(d).

(h) *To borrow*, on the security of the Company's assets, any money which may be needed (s.245(2)(e)), e.g. by mortgage of land,

[1] *Re F. T. Hawkins & Company Limited* [1952] 2 All E.R. 467.

[2] [1966] 1 W.L.R. 1450.

[3] *Plant Engineers (Sales) Limited* v *Davis* (1969) 113 *Sol. J.* 484.

but not so as to take priority over existing secured lenders whose rights are already fixed.[1]

(i) To take out, in his official name, *Letters of Administration* to the estate of any deceased contributory: s.245(2)(f).

(j) To appoint an *agent* to do any business which he cannot do himself: s.245(2)(g).

(k) *To do all such things as may be necessary* for winding-up the affairs of the Company, and distributing its assets: s.245(2)(h). This may give the Liquidator a power to lease the Company's property if it is necessary for the purposes of the Winding-Up.

(2) The three particular powers, which are set out in s.245, but which are excluded from the overall authority given by s.303(1)(a) are the following:

(a) To *pay any class of Creditors in full.*

(b) To *make compromises with Creditors.*

(c) To *make compromises with contributories* and other debtors.

These powers can only be exercised by the Liquidator in a Voluntary Winding-Up with the sanction of:

(a) an extraordinary resolution (i.e. 75% majority) of the Company, in a Members' Winding-Up, or

(b) the Court, or the Committee of Inspection or (if there is no Committee) an ordinary resolution of the Creditors, in a Creditors' Winding-Up: s.303(1)(a).

(3) Certain additional powers are given to voluntary Liquidators by s.303 and may be exercised *without sanction.* These are:

(a) To settle the lists of contributories: s.303(1)(c).

(b) To make calls: s.303(1)(d).

(c) To summon meetings of the Company for any purpose: s.303(1)(e).

(d) To pay the debts of the Company and to adjust the rights of the contributories among themselves: s.303(2).

(4) Certain other sections give further specific powers:

(a) To summon meetings of the Creditors to ascertain their wishes: (s.246(2)).

(b) To call meetings of the Committee of Inspection where necessary: s.253(2).

(c) To rectify the Register of Members, where the Liquidator sanctions transfers: s.282.

[1] *Re Regent's Canal Ironworks Company* [1875] 3 Ch. D. 411.

(d) To sanction, in a Members' Winding-Up, the continued exercise of the powers of the Directors, either generally or for any specific purpose: s.285(2).
The Liquidator shares this power with the Company in general meeting.

(e) Reconstruction and sale under s.287: with the sanction of a special resolution (i.e. 75% majority) of the Company (with the additional sanction of the Court or Committee of Inspection in a Creditors' Winding-Up, s.298) the Liquidator has power to *sell the assets of the Company in exchange for shares* in another company, for distribution among the members: s.287(1).
In relation to the exercise of the powers conferred by s.287 it should be noted that:
  (i) A sale is binding on the members of the transferor Company: s.287(2).
  (ii) Any dissentient who did not vote for the special resolution may, within seven days, require the Liquidator either to abstain from carrying it into effect or to purchase his interest at a price to be agreed or fixed by arbitration: s.287(3).
  (iii) If, within a year, a Winding-Up Order is made the special resolution is void unless sanctioned by the Court: s.287(5).

(f) To *distribute the property* of the Company among the members in accordance with their rights, after discharging preferential debts and thereafter other liabilities of the Company *pari passu*: (s.302).

(g) *To apply to the Court* to have any question in the Winding-Up determined: s.307.
This power is shared with the contributories and Creditors. If the Liquidator is in any doubt as to the proper course he should take he should apply to the Court because good faith alone will not necessarily render him immune from suit at the instance of persons aggrieved by *his actions.*[1]
Under Section 307, the Court can exercise all the powers which it would have in a Compulsory Winding-Up. The Court, if satisfied that the determination of a question referred to it or the exercise of any of its powers will be just and beneficial, may make such order as it thinks fit: s.307(2).
It is the practice of the Court to deal only with specific

[1] See for example *Re Home & Colonial Insurance Company* [1930] 1 Ch. 102.

requests, raised on motion or by summons.[1] Applications in the first instance are dealt with by the Registrar in Chambers although they may be adjourned to the Judge as and when required (Rules 4–7).

(h) *With the leave of the Court, to disclaim* land burdened with onerous covenants, unprofitable contracts, or any other property that is unsaleable or not readily saleable: (s.323). It should be noted that:

(i) The object of section 323 is to enable the Liquidator to get rid of worthless or burdensome contracts of the Company which could delay or prejudice the Winding-Up. Third parties injured by the operation of a disclaimer are deemed to be Creditors of the Company and can prove in the Winding-Up for the amount of their injury: (s.323(7)).

(ii) The power to disclaim must be exercised in writing by the Liquidator within twelve months of the commencement of the Winding-Up or, unless the Liquidator seems certain of the property within one month from such commencement becomes available within twelve months of the date when he first became aware of the property, unless the Court extends the period: (s.323(1)).

(iii) Any person interested can require the Liquidator to decide within twenty-eight days whether or not he will disclaim. If within that time (or such further period as the Court may allow) he does not give notice that he intends to apply to the Court, the Liquidator loses the right to disclaim: s.323(4).

(iv) Section 323 applies to land burdened with onerous covenants, stocks or shares, unprofitable contracts or any other property that is unsaleable or not readily saleable because of onerous obligations, e.g. land held by a cemetery company with covenants giving certain persons exclusive rights of burial[2], and it applies even though the Liquidator has taken possession, or endeavoured to sell.

(v) The Court can make orders on the application of any person interested, rescinding a contract made with the Company on such terms as it thinks fit, or vesting any

[1] *Re Union Bank of Kingston-upon-Hull* (1880) 13 Ch. D. 808.
[2] *Re Nottingham General Cemetery Co.* [1955] Ch. 683.

disclaimed property in such persons as it may decide: s.323(5) and (6).

In the case of leaseholds, the person in whom the Court vests the lease, whether as underlessee or mortgagee, will take subject to all the liabilities which bound the Company: s.323(6)(a).

If such persons refuse to accept the Court's terms they may lose all their rights in the leasehold property, which can then be vested by the Court in any person that it thinks fit.

(vi) The procedure is to apply to the Court ex parte by summons supported by an affidavit stating the parties interested and their interests: Rule 75.

The forms of disclaimer are Forms 35 and 36 in the Appendix to the Rules (see page 178 post). The Court may not allow the power to be exercised so as to prejudice third parties unfairly, e.g. where it would operate to release guarantors from their obligations under a lease.[1]

(vii) Where a Liquidator retains leasehold property for the benefit or convenience of the Winding-Up and thereafter disclaims, the landlord may be entitled to be paid out of the assets of the Company in liquidation the full amount of any rent becoming due during the period of such retention.[2]

(viii) Where a Liquidator adopts or implements a contract with the Company he may by his conduct be precluded thereafter from obtaining leave to disclaim. Thus where a company had entered into a contract for the purchase of a house and the Liquidator instructed the vendor's solicitors who were also acting for the Company to 'proceed with the transfer' he was thereafter refused leave to disclaim.[3]

[1] *Re Katherine et Cie* [1932] 1 Ch. 70.

[2] *Re ABC Coupler & Engineering Co. Ltd.* (No. 3) [1970] 1 W.L.R. 702; see pp. 54–55 post.

[3] *Boston House Property Co. Ltd.* v *Ludgate Finance Company Limited* (1966) 110 Sol. J. 768.

CHAPTER 7

Creditors

Duty to Creditors

As appears from p 11 *ante* the Liquidator is in some respects a trustee for the general body of the Creditors of the Company, although not for any individual Creditor.[1] He may be liable for negligence if he does not properly perform his duties, e.g. if he pays money to a Creditor whose claim is invalid[2] or distributes the assets without providing for a contingent liability for rent.[3] Furthermore, the Liquidator may be restrained from making a distribution if there are liabilities (e.g. possible claims by employees) which are still to be ascertained.[4] Performance of these duties can be enforced by a misfeasance summons under s.333, although the Court has a discretion as to the amount of any compensation to be paid by the Liquidator, and may only, for example, order the Liquidator to provide enough to pay the Company's Creditors.[5]

Procedure

On taking up his appointment, the Liquidator will have before him either the statement of assets and liabilities in the Declaration of Solvency, if there is one (see Form 1 on page 126), or the Statement of Affairs and List of Creditors laid before the Creditors' meeting (see Form 3 on page 129). The steps which he would normally take thereafter are as follows:

(1) To *write to every Creditor* known to him, informing them of his appointment, of the constitution of the Committee of Inspection (if any) and inviting them to submit details of their claims (not proofs at this stage). (Specimen letter on page 141). Accompanying this first letter will be:
   (a) Copy of the *Statement of Affairs*.

[1] *Knowles* v *Scott* [1891] 1 Ch. 717.
[2] *Re J. Russell Electronics Limited* [1968] 1 W.L.R. 1252.
[3] *James Smith & Sons (Norwood) Limited* v *Goodman* [1936] Ch. 216.
[4] *Re Armstrong Whitworth Securities Limited* [1947] Ch. 673.
[5] *Re V.G.M. Holdings* [1942] Ch. 235.

(b) Copy *List of Creditors.*

(c) *Formal Notice to Claim.*

Rule 106 requires the Liquidator to send this notice in the case of a Voluntary Winding-Up to each person who to the knowledge of the Liquidator claims to be a Creditor or Preferential Creditor of the Company and whose claim has not been admitted.

It has been held that the fact that the Liquidator had *advertised* for Creditors will not avail him if, in fact, he knows of other Creditors, and has failed to give them notice.[1] The date by which debts are to be proved will be the same as that stated in the advertisement (see (2) below). It will be not less than fourteen days and, in practice, at least one month after the notice. (See Forms 3 and 153 on pp. 129, 143).

(2) The Formal Notice to Claim will be *advertised* "in such newspaper as he shall consider convenient" (Rule 106(2)), normally the *Gazette* and one local paper. (See Form 15A on page 142.)

The notice requires Creditors to submit details of their debts and any claims to priority, to the Liquidator by a fixed date (not less than fourteen days after the notice), failing which they will be excluded in accordance with the provisions of rule 106 from the benefit of any distribution made before the debts are proved. The Liquidator ought not to disregard claims of which he knows merely because they are not submitted or proved within the stated time. The least which he should do in such cases is to give the Creditor a further and final notice to prove. Otherwise the Liquidator could find himself being called upon to pay such claims personally,[2] and indeed, the only course of complete safety is for the Liquidator to obtain an order permitting him to distribute without reference to the unproved claims. The Court is unlikely to allow a Creditor, who has received two notices, to disturb existing dividends, although he will always be allowed to prove if there are funds available.[3] However, a Creditor who has omitted to prove will be precluded from sharing in any distribution after surplus assets have been paid to the contributories and the company dissolved.[4]

[1] See *Re Armstrong Whitworth Securities Limited* [1947] Ch. 673.

[2] *Ibid.*

[3] *Harrison* v *Kirk* [1904] A.C. 1. HL.

[4] *Butler* v *Broadhead* [1975] Ch. 97.

(3) The Liquidator will then receive written statements of claim from the Creditors. The common form of Notice to Claim envisages that the Creditors or their solicitors will "come in and prove", i.e. attend in person before the Liquidator and prove their debts. This is not what happens in practice. Rule 92(2) (as amended in 1977) allows any debt to be proved by delivering or posting to the Liquidator in a pre-paid letter an unsworn claim to the debt or an affidavit verifying the debt as the Liquidator may direct. Whether the Liquidator should require an affidavit verifying the debt or simply be satisfied with an unsworn claim will entirely depend upon the circumstances of each particular claim. Where the Liquidator is in any doubt concerning the validity of a claim he should require an affidavit to be sworn. (Forms of proof are on pp. 146 and 148 *post*). If a Creditor, who according to the Company's books may have a good claim, takes no steps to make such a claim, the Liquidator is not entitled to admit a debt to that Creditor merely because the debt appears in the Company's books.[1]

(4) The Liquidator must then *examine every proof* and claim to priority which he receives and admit or reject it in writing, or require further evidence. If he rejects a proof he must state his grounds in writing to the Creditor. (Form 17 on page 149: Rule 107).
There is no time limit for admission or rejection, although twenty-eight days is fixed for a Compulsory Winding-Up by Rule 117. Dealing with proofs is one of the most important of a Liquidator's tasks and a Liquidator may be personally liable if he admits an unfounded claim. In the leading case of *Re The Home & Colonial Insurance Company Limited*[2] the Liquidator accepted insurance "slips" as evidence of debts, in accordance with a common practice in the field of reinsurance contracts. He therefore paid the large sum which was being claimed on these slips, but it was subsequently held that the slips did not conform to the provisions of the Stamp and Marine Insurance Acts and that there had been no legal liability to pay. As the Company would otherwise have been solvent, the Liquidator was held personally liable to pay sufficient to enable all the Creditors to be paid in full with interest at 5%.

[1] *Re Compania de Electricidad de la Provincia de Buenos Aires Ltd.* [1980] Ch. 146.
[2] [1930] 1 Ch. 102.

(5) Any Creditor whose proof is rejected has the right under Rule 108 to *appeal* to the Court to reverse or vary the decision. Although there is no express time limit in a Voluntary Winding-Up, twenty-one days is specified in the case of a Compulsory Winding-Up (Rule 108), and save in exceptional circumstances the Court will not permit a Creditor to pursue his appeal unless he has proceeded with reasonable despatch after notice of registration.

(6) The Liquidator, or any Creditor or contributory, have a similar right to apply to the Court to expunge or reduce a proof, if they think that it has been wrongly admitted: Rules 109–110.

(7) The Liquidator may be faced with the question of what to do about Creditors who have failed to prove or who have taken no steps to dispute his rejection of their proof. As a last resort he can apply to the Court under s.307 for an order under s.264, excluding Creditors whose debts are not proved within a specified time. In practice the Liquidator has a duty to ascertain by direct enquiry whether claims are being pressed. The right course should be to give a further notice to such Creditors that unless they prove or apply to the Court within a specified date, e.g. one month, he will distribute, without regard to their claims. The Court would be unlikely to allow such Creditors to upset any dividend which was then paid.[1] However, where there has been delay by the solicitors for both parties in dealing with a Creditor's claim, the Liquidator cannot use this as an excuse to exclude a Creditor from a distribution.[2]

Debts which are provable

In examining claims the Liquidator must bear in mind the following general principles:

(1) *If the Company is Solvent*
All debts are provable whether contingent or certain, present or future, ascertained or sounding only in damages: s.316, i.e. all debts are provable which could have been enforced against the Company before it went into liquidation or which might ultimately have become enforceable but not for example:

[1] *Re General Rolling Stock Company* (1872) 7 Ch. App. 646.
[2] *Austin Securities Limited* v *Northgate & English Stores Ltd.* [1969] 1 W.L.R. 529.

(a) Voluntary pensions;[1]
(b) Debts arising from ultra vires contracts,[2] and
(c) Statute-barred debts, unless the shareholders all consent[3], though an acknowledgement of a debt in the Balance Sheet may in some circumstances prevent time from running.[4]

Contingent or unascertained claims must be proved on the basis of a "just estimate": s.316. Examples of such claims are a landlord's claim for future rent which would have fallen due to him under a Lease[5] and a sales representative's claim for a fair proportion of his estimated loss of commission.[6] However, Rule 101 requires a rebate to be deducted of 5% per annum up to the date when the debts would have become payable.

In the case of a solvent company, the Creditors will of course be paid in full, and the order of payment is therefore of less importance; there must, however, be no distribution to the members until all the debts have been paid, and if in doubt, the Liquidator should proceed on the basis that the Company is insolvent. The principle is that a company in liquidation is regarded as insolvent until the contrary is proved,[7] or becomes obvious.[8]

(2) *If the Company is Insolvent*

The general rule is that the provisions of *Bankruptcy Law* apply (s.317), *including* those relating to:
(a) The debts provable;[9]
(b) The rights of secured and unsecured Creditors;
(c) The valuation of uncertain and contingent liabilities;
(d) Set-off;
(e) Interest on debts;[10]

but *excluding* the rules as to:

[1] *Re Birkbeck P. B. Building Society* [1913] 1 Ch. 400.
[2] *Re Jon Beauforte (London) Limited* [1953] 1 Ch. 131, but see the European Communities Act 1972, Section 9.
[3] *Re Art Reproduction Company* [1952] Ch. 89.
[4] *Jones* v *Bellegrove Properties Limited* [1949] 2 K.B. 700; *Re Gee & Co. (Woolwich) Ltd.* [1975] Ch. 52; *Re Compania de Electricidad de la Provincia de Buenos Aires Ltd.* [1980] Ch. 146.
[5] *James Smith & Sons (Norwood) Limited* v *Goodman* [1936] Ch. 216.
[6] *Re Patent Floor Cloth Company* (1872) 26 L.T. 476.
[7] *Re Milan Tramways Company* (1884) 25 Ch. D. 587.
[8] *Re Fine Industrial Commodities Limited* [1956] Ch. 256.
[9] But see *post* p. 47 in relation to tort claims.
[10] *Re Theo. Garvin Ltd.* [1969] 1 Ch. 624.

(a) Reputed ownership (s.38(3) Bankruptcy Act 1914), which in some circumstances gives the Creditors a better title to property in the possession of a bankrupt than he had himself;[1]

(b) The right of Landlords to distrain for rent due before the Winding-Up;[2]

(c) Limitation of power of Trustee in Bankruptcy as to Copyright.[3]

The essential difference between insolvent and solvent companies, so far as provable debts are concerned, is that *claims* for *unliquidated damages* cannot be proved in an insolvent liquidation *unless* they arise by reason of a *contract, promise* or *breach of trust*: Bankruptcy Act 1914, s.30.

Damages for tort not liquidated by judgement or agreement before the commencement of the Winding-Up are excluded from proof for so long as they remain unliquidated. However in *re Berkeley Securities* (*Property*) *Ltd*[4] it was recently held that damages for tort which became liquidated after the commencement of the Winding-Up were provable against those assets remaining undistributed.

(3) *Secured Creditors*

Secured Creditors, i.e. those who have some mortgage, charge or lien on the Company's property, have various alternatives:

(a) To rely on their security if they consider that it is worth more than the debt, and not prove in the liquidation;

(b) To realise the security and prove for any balance;

(c) To value the security and prove for any balance, in which case the Liquidator can redeem at the valuation;

(d) To surrender the security and prove for the whole debt: Bankruptcy Act 1914, Sch. II.

A landlord's power of distress does not make him a secured Creditor, but a solicitor's lien on documents does have this effect and it must be disclosed in his proof, even though he may be unable to value or realise his security.[5]

Any security held must be disclosed in a Creditor's proof (Rule 95) and he only votes in respect of any unsecured balance (Rule 141). If he votes in respect of the whole debt, he may be

[1] *Re Crumlin Viaduct Works Company* [1879] 11 Ch. D. 755.

[2] *Re Coal Consumers' Association* (1876) 3 Ch. D. 625.

[3] *Re Health Promotion Limited* [1932] 1 Ch. 65.

[4] [1980] 3 All E.R. 513 *Vinelott J.*

[5] *Re Safety Explosives Limited* [1904] 1 Ch. 226.

deemed to have surrendered his security, unless the Court decides that it was due to inadvertence: Rule 141.

The Liquidator may, within twenty-eight days after a proof or statement estimating the value of a security has been used for voting at a meeting, require the Creditor to give up the security on payment of the value so estimated with an addition thereto of 20% (Rule 142).

(4) *Invalid Securities*

When dealing with secured Creditors, the Liquidator must satisfy himself as to the validity of their security.

Several factors may be relevant:

(a) Almost all *charges* given by a company must be *registered* with the Registrar of Companies *within twenty-one* days of their creation: s.95; and if not so registered, are *void* against the Liquidator and Creditors. Failure to register converts the holder of such a charge into an ordinary unsecured Creditor. When a charge becomes void under s.95 the money secured thereby becomes immediately repayable.

The Liquidator should, therefore, check every such charge on which a Creditor relies against the file maintained by the Registrar of Companies to ascertain whether the charge has been duly registered. It should be noted that the twenty-one days' period runs from the date when the charge is created, i.e. executed, and not from the time when the advance is made or the charge dated, if dated after execution.[1]

A problem arises where the Liquidator ascertains that a charge requiring registration under s.95 has in fact been registered more than twenty-one days after its creation (time for registration not having been extended under s.101). In such circumstances the Registrar's certificate of registration is conclusive evidence that all the requirements of the Act as to registration have been complied with.[2] However, if it can positively be shown that Creditors have been misled into giving credit to the Company between the dates when the charge should have been registered and when it was in fact registered, the

[1] *Esberger & Son Limited* v *Capital & Counties Bank* [1913] 2 Ch. 366.

[2] *Re C.L. Nye Ltd.* [1971] 1 Ch. 442; cf s. 98(2).

chargee may be precluded from taking full advantage of his security.[1]

In addition to investigation of registration the Liquidator will need to examine the charge itself to ascertain the total amount secured as the charge can extend to sums beyond those mentioned in the registration.[2]

(b) An unpaid vendor's lien arising by operation of law does not require registration under s.95.[3] However, where pursuant to an agreement an unpaid vendor is to have a charge over the property sold, including a charge arising by way of deposit of title deeds,[4] such a charge is registrable under s.95. Furthermore, where such a charge is avoided for non-registration, the unpaid vendor's lien does not thereafter revive.[5]

(c) Certain *Floating Charges* may be void even if duly registered: s.322.

This section provides that if a floating charge is created within twelve months of commencement of Winding-Up it is void, except as to the amount of any cash paid to the Company at the time of or subsequently to the creation of and in consideration for the charge, together with interest therein at 5% per annum, unless it is proved that the Company immediately after the creation of the charge was solvent. The meaning of "cash paid at the time of or subsequently to and in consideration to the charge" has been the subject of a number of judicial decisions. Thus it has been held:

(i) that money advanced a few days before the charge, but in reliance on a promise to execute it, is money paid "at the time";[6]

(ii) that cash must have been received by the Company "to do what it liked with",[7] and that the test is whether in substance as well as in form, the payment was intended to benefit the Company and not some other person;[8]

[1] See *ibid per Harman LJ* at p. 470–471.

[2] *Re Mechanisations (Eaglescliffe) Limited* [1966] Ch. 20.

[3] *London & Cheshire Insurance Company Limited* v *Laplagrene Property Company Limited* [1971] Ch. 499.

[4] *Re Wallis & Simmonds (Builders) Ltd.* [1974] 1 W.L.R. 391.

[5] *Burston Finance Ltd.* v *Speirway Ltd.* [1974] 1 W.L.R. 1648.

[6] *Re Columbian Fireproofing Company Limited* [1910] 2 Ch. 120.

[7] *Re Orleans Motor Company Limited* [1911] 2 Ch. 41.

[8] *Re Ambassadors Hotel (Bournemouth) Limited* (1961) 105 Sol. J. 969.

(iii) that where cheques are paid by a bank to third parties from an existing overdraft secured by a floating charge, the rule in *Clayton's Case*[1] (First-In, First-Out) applies so that subsequent payments in can be set against the earlier indebtedness. This leaves the later advances secured by the charge, which are made "in consideration of the fact that the charge exists" even though the Bank was under no obligation to make them;[2]

(iv) that whether or not the Company was solvent immediately after the charge was created depends on whether it could pay its debts as they fell due. A surplus of assets over liabilities is not decisive.[3]
It is only the charge which is invalidated by s.322. To the extent of the invalidity, the Creditor ranks with the ordinary unsecured Creditors.

(d) If the borrowing is *ULTRA VIRES,* the loan and the securities are void, the lender cannot sue and the Liquidator must not pay him voluntarily since this is not a legally binding debt.
Trading companies, however, have implied power to borrow and give security for their trading purposes, and borrowing is only likely to cause difficulty if it is for a purpose outside the permitted objects. In these circumstances, the loan (and the charge) will be invalid only if the lender knew that it was for an ultra vires purpose.[4]
If the indebtedness secured by a charge arises from an ultra vires transaction unless the Creditor is able to claim the benefit of section 9(1) of the European Communities Act 1972, the charge will be invalid and the Creditor will be unable to rely upon his security.

(e) If a charge has been created within six months of the passing of the resolution for Voluntary Winding-Up and in such circumstances as to amount to a fraudulent preference it will be void against the Liquidator.[5]

(5) *Reservation of Title Clauses*
Many suppliers of goods to a company now include in their

[1] (1816) 1 Mer. 572.
[2] *Re Yeovil Glove Company Limited* [1964] Ch. 148.
[3] *Re Patrick & Lyon Limited* [1933] 1 Ch. 786.
[4] *Re Jon Beauforte (London) Limited* [1953] Ch. 131; Re Introductions Ltd. [1970] Ch. 99.
[5] See pp. 32, 33 *ante*.

conditions of supply a clause retaining title to such goods until payment has been made in full. Such a clause will generally be effective against a Liquidator in respect of the original goods supplied, if still in existence. Where, however, such a clause also seeks to obtain for the supplier any rights over the proceeds of sale of the goods or any product incorporating the goods such additional rights may be invalid against the Liquidator, e.g. for failure to register under s.95. In each case the effectiveness of any reservation of title clause will depend upon its proper construction.[1]

(6) *Compromises and Arrangements*

Compromises and arrangements with Creditors can be made in three ways:

(i) *Under s.306* an arrangement is binding on the Company if sanctioned by an extraordinary resolution and on the Creditors if agreed by three-quarters in number and value. Any objector (member or Creditor) can appeal to the Court within three weeks.

This section only applies to a company which is about to be, or is in the course of being, wound-up.

(ii) *Under s.206* any company can enter into a binding compromise or arrangement with its Creditors or members or any class of either under a *Scheme of Arrangement approved by the Court* and by a majority in number and three-quarters in value of those affected.

These sections are discussed in conjunction with a Voluntary Winding-Up and Sale under s.287 at pp. 77, 78 *post*.

(iii) *Under s.303(1)(a)* incorporating *s.245(1)(e)* the *Liquidator can himself make compromises* or arrangements with Creditors, with the sanction of an extraordinary resolution of the Company in a Members' Winding-Up or consent of the Court, or the Committee of Inspection (or, if none, the Creditors) in a Creditors' Winding-Up.

(7) *Costs and Interest on Debts*

(a) The *cost* of proving a debt is born by the *Creditor* unless the Court otherwise orders (Rule 97), and in making up

[1] See *Aluminium Industrie Vaassen BV* v *Romalpa Aluminium Ltd.* [1976] 1 W.L.R. 676; *Re Bond Worth Ltd.* [1979] 3 W.L.R. 629; *Borden (U.K.) Ltd.* v *Scottish Timber Products Ltd.* [1979] 3 W.L.R. 672.

his proof, the Creditor must, moreover, deduct any cash *discount* which he may have agreed in excess of 5% on the amount of his claim and any trade discount (Rule 98). Where a creditor brings an action after receiving notice of the Winding-Up except in special circumstances the Creditor will not be allowed to include the costs of the action in his proof.[1]

(b) *Interest*

(i) If the Company is *insolvent*, interest ceases to run in all cases (except for secured Creditors) at the date of commencement of Winding-Up.[2]

(ii) Up to the date of Winding-Up, interest, if due at an agreed rate, is provable at that rate, but the Creditor only receives dividends on such interest at a rate not exceeding 5% per annum until all the provable debts have been paid in full. It was held in *Re Theo. Garvin Limited*[3] that the Bankruptcy rule to this effect (s.66(1) Bankruptcy Act 1914 applies to an insolvent company.

(iii) If the debt is due at a certain date under a written instrument, interest runs at 4% from that date until commencement of Winding-Up (Rule 100). A creditor's standard form invoice (which amounts to a statement of account only) is not a written instrument for the purposes of Rule 100.[4]

(iv) Otherwise, interest runs at 4% from the date of demand in writing, requiring interest (Rule 100).

(v) If the Company is *solvent,* interest after the commencement of the Winding-Up may be claimed up to the date of payment if the Creditor is entitled to it.[5] However, as the Company is solvent a creditor cannot claim a right to be paid statutory interest of 4% per annum as in the case of a bankruptcy (s.33(8) Bankruptcy Act 1914) out of surplus assets since the bankruptcy rules only apply to insolvent companies and not to solvent companies.[6]

[1] *Rose* v *Garden Lodge Coal Company* (1878) 3 Q.B.D. 235.

[2] *Re Thomas Salt & Company Ltd.* (1908) 28 L.T. 558.

[3] [1969] 1 Ch. 624 approved in *Re Jessel Securities Limited* (21st December 1978) unreported (C.A.).

[4] *Re Rolls Royce Co. Ltd.* [1974] 1 W.L.R. 1584.

[5] *Re W. W. Duncan & Company* [1905] 1 Ch. 307.

[6] *Re Rolls Royce Co. Ltd. supra.*

(8) *Set-Off*

The Bankruptcy rules (Bankruptcy Act 1914, s.31) are applied to the Winding-Up of insolvent companies by s.317.

(a) Where there have been mutual dealings, sums due from the one must be set off against those due from the other and only the balance can be claimed on either side (Bankruptcy Act 1914, s.31). The provisions of s.31 are mandatory and cannot be excluded by agreement.[1]

(b) For a set-off to exist, the two claims may be of different types but they must be "mutual" or "commensurable" and resolve themselves into *money payments,* e.g. a claim for the return of goods will not suffice.[2]

(c) The claims must arise in the same right, i.e. the person beneficially entitled or obligated must be the same in all the claims which are to be set-off.[3]

(d) No one can claim the right of set-off if, at the time of giving credit, he knew that the Company had committed the equivalent of an available act of bankruptcy committed by an individual, e.g. the sending out of a notice under s.293.[4]

(e) The account must be taken at the date of commencement of the Winding-Up and new transactions after that date, e.g. goods sold by the Liquidator, are excluded—but not transactions which originated before that date.[5]

(f) If the Company is solvent the ordinary law as to set-off applies and not the Bankruptcy rules.

(9) *Landlords and Distress*

(a) A landlord is not a secured or preferential Creditor but his position differs from that of other Creditors in some respects.

(b) Most rack-rent leases (as opposed to leases at a ground rent) contain provisions for forfeiture and re-entry if the tenant goes into liquidation, otherwise than for amalgamation or reconstruction. If the Landlord takes advantage of this provision and the lease is of value the Liquidator will wish to save it:

[1] *Halesowen Presswork & Assemblies Ltd.* v *Westminster Bank Ltd.* [1972] A.C. 785.

[2] *Eberle's Hotel Company Limited* v *Jonas* (1887) 18 Q.B. 459; *Rolls Razor Limited* v *Cox* [1967] Q.B. 552.

[3] *Re Brown & Gregory Limited* [1904] 1 Ch. 627.

[4] *Re Eros Films Limited* [1963] Ch. 565.

[5] *Re Daintrey* [1900] Q.B. 546.

(i) If the Landlord seeks to forfeit under these provisions notice must be served and the Liquidator can generally apply for relief against forfeiture *within one year* from the commencement of the Winding-Up (Law of Property Act 1925, s.146(10)) and the Court can grant or refuse the application as it thinks fit. The one year limitation does not apply where in the course of that year the Company's interest as lessee is sold.[1]

(ii) If the Landlord actually takes possession, which he is entitled to do, if he can do so peaceably, it may then be too late to apply for relief.[2]

(iii) If the Landlord seeks to forfeit for *non-payment of rent* (which is excluded from L.P.A., s.146) no notice is required, but the Tenant has a right to apply for relief on payment of all arrears and costs. The Liquidator must apply within *six months* of the execution of the Landlord's judgement for possession.

(iv) If the Landlord takes *possession peaceably* and without recourse to the Court, for *non-payment of rent,* the Liquidator may, in this case, be able to obtain relief[3] and it has been held that as the granting of relief in this case is equitable, the six months' time limit is not applicable.[4]

(c) *Distress* for rent is the Landlord's specific remedy and it entitles him to seize and sell goods on the premises, without recourse to the Court.
In a Compulsory Winding-Up the Landlord is postponed to the preferential Creditors in respect of distress levied by him within the three months before the order (s.319(7)). This provision does not apply to a Voluntary Liquidation and distress levied before the date of the resolution will not be interfered with by the Court unless it can be shown that the Landlord has been guilty of unconsionable conduct.[5]

(d) Distress after Winding-Up is void in a Compulsory Winding-Up (s.228), and although this is not so in a

[1] *Pearson* v *Gee and Braceborough Spa Ltd.* [1934] A.C. 272.
[2] *Rogers* v *Rice* [1892] 2 Ch. 170.
[3] *Lovelock* v *Margo* [1963] 2 Q.B. 786.
[4] *Thatcher* v *L. H. Pearce & Sons (Contractors)* [1968] 1 W.L.R. 748.
[5] *Re Roundwood Colliery Company* [1897] 1 Ch. 373; *Re Herbert Berry Associates Limited* [1977] 1 W.L.R. 1437.

Voluntary Winding-Up, the Court will normally restrain the Landlord from levying charges in respect of rent due before the Winding-Up leaving him with his right of proof.[1]

(e) Rent due after the Winding-Up may be distrained for, if the Court is satisfied that possession has been retained for the benefit of the Liquidation,[2] but not where it has been retained with the Landlord's acquiescence, for the benefit of all parties.[3] If he does retain possession for the purposes of the liquidation, the Liquidator must pay the rent in full for his period of occupation[4] out of the assets of the Company and perform the other covenants, e.g. repairing.[5]

(f) Where the Landlord has no direct right of proof, e.g. because the Company is an under-lessee, he will not be restrained from distraining.[6]

(g) Where the Liquidator does not take possession, failing distress or forfeiture, the Landlord's only remedy is to *prove for the rent,* and breaches of covenant, including any claim for future rent, under s.316.[7]

(h) The Liquidator must bear in mind that there may be a contingent liability not only under the Company's own leases, but under other leases, which it has at any time held. Thus, if it was an original lessee, it remains, in effect, a guarantor of the rent for the whole term; if it took an assignment, it remains liable to indemnify the assignor if the present Tenant defaults.

The Liquidator may render himself personally liable if he distributes the assets without regard to these contingent claims and he can be restrained if he tries to do so,[8] and a fund can be ordered to be set aside.

It may be extremely difficult to quantify these liabilities, but the prospective Creditors should be given notice and

[1] *Re South Rhondda Colliery Company* [1928] W.N. 126.

[2] *Re Lundy Granite Company* (1871) 6 Ch. App. 462.

[3] *Re Progress Assurance Company* (1870) L.R. 9 Eq. 370.

[4] *Re Oak Pitts Colliery Company* (1882) 21 Ch. D. 322 and Rule 99; *Re Downer Enterprises Ltd.* [1974] 1 W.L.R. 1460; *Re ABC Coupler & Engineering Co. Ltd. (No. 3)* [1970] 1 W.L.R. 702.

[5] *Re Levi & Company* [1911] 1 Ch. 416.

[6] *Re Regent United Services Stores* (1878) 8 Ch. D. 616.

[7] *James Smith & Sons (Norwood) Limited* v *Goodman* [1936] Ch. 216.

[8] *Oppenheimer* v *British Bank* [1877] 6 Ch. D. 744.

an opportunity to prove. Similar principles apply where a company is seeking to return paid-up capital to its shareholders and in one case it was decided that a fund equivalent to ten years' rent should be set aside.[1] However, it has been held that a landlord is not entitled as of right to have a fund set aside in this way.[2]

(i) If the Lease is burdened with onerous covenants the Liquidator can apply to the Court for *leave to disclaim* under s.323, in which case the liability for rent and repairs will cease, but the Landlord will be entitled to prove for the loss which he has suffered. This will enable the contingent claim to be quantified.[3]

[1] *Re Lucania Temperance Billiard Hall (London) Limited* [1966] Ch. 98.
[2] *Re House Property & Investment Company Limited* [1954] Ch. 576.
[3] *Re McEwan* (1875) 11 Ch. D. 572 and see p. 55 *ante*.

CHAPTER 8

Committee of Inspection and Meetings

(1) In *a Members' Winding-Up,* control remains in the hands of the *members,* there are no meetings of Creditors except under ss. 288 and 291 (since they must all be paid in full) and no Committee of Inspection will be appointed.
The wishes of the members are ascertained in general meetings summoned in the manner required by the Articles or s. 134. The Liquidator can call such meetings at any time (s. 303(1)(e)) and must call one for the following purposes:
- (i) To fix the Liquidator's remuneration (ordinary resolution): s.285(1).
- (ii) To fill a vacancy in the office of Liquidator (ordinary resolution): s.286.
- (iii) To pay any class of Creditors in full, to make compromises with Creditors or to make compromises with members and other debtors (extraordinary resolution): s.303(1)(a).
- (iv) To sell the assets in exchange for shares in another company (special resolution): s.287.
- (v) To authorise the disposal of the books and papers at the conclusion of the Winding-Up (extraordinary resolution): s.341(b).
- (vi) To receive an account of the Liquidator's acts and dealings and of the conduct of the liquidation within three months of the end of the first year of the liquidation and each succeeding year: s.289.

Although "contributories" replace "members" as the parties interested in a Members' Winding-Up, the meetings referred to above are conducted on the same basis as if the Company were not in liquidation. It therefore appears that only members on the register are entitled to attend and vote. Although Rule 128 provides that the Winding-Up Rules as to meetings apply generally to all Winding-Up Meetings, the main heading to that part of the Rules dealing with meetings (Rules 127–145) seems to specifically exclude members' meetings in a Members' Winding-Up.[1] The heading reads: "General Meetings of Creditors and Contributories in relation to Winding-Up by the Court and of Creditors in relation to a Creditor's Voluntary Winding-Up." Bearing in mind that in the case of a solvent company, where the debts are bound to be paid in full, those contributories who are not on the Register, i.e. past members, will have no interest in the liquidation, and their exclusion from meetings would be logical.

(2) *In a Creditors' Winding-Up*, control passes to the Creditors and their nominees.
The Company may, at its Winding-Up meeting, have nominated up to five members for a *Committee of Inspection*; the Creditors at their meeting may likewise appoint up to five members and *may exclude* the Company's nominees, unless the Court orders otherwise: s.295.
In practice the Liquidator will usually want to see a Committee of Inspection appointed, as otherwise he will have to call meetings of the Creditors to exercise the powers which the Committee could have exercised. The object of appointing a Committee of Inspection is to provide a representative body to assist and supervise the Liquidator. Section 253 applies to their proceedings as in a Compulsory Winding-Up: s.295(2) (except for s.253(1), which provides for the constitution and appointment of the Committee in a Compulsory Winding-Up).
Proceedings of the Committee of Inspection are governed by the following rules (s.253):
   (i) It meets as and when it appoints or when called by the Liquidator or any member and failing such appointment, at least once a month: s.253(2).
   (ii) A majority of the Committee forms a quorum: s.253(3).
   (iii) The Committee acts by a majority of those present: s.253(3).
   (iv) A member vacates office if he resigns in writing, becomes bankrupt, is absent from five consecutive meetings without leave, or is removed by ordinary resolution of those who appointed him: s.253(4)(5)(6).
   (v) On a vacancy occurring, the Liquidator must call a meeting of the appropriate body to fill it, unless he

[1] Cf Rule 2(2).

considers that this is unnecessary in which case he can apply to the Court for an order that the vacancy should not be filled or alternatively should not be filled save in such circumstances as the Court may specify: s.253(7).

(vi) If the continuing members are at least two, they may act, despite any vacancy: s.253(8).

Members of the Committee are in a fiduciary position and neither they nor the Liquidator may purchase any part of the Company's assets except with the consent of the Court: (Rule 161). The members of the Committee may not make any profit out of any transaction arising in the course of the Winding-Up[1] nor receive out of the Company's assets any remuneration for services rendered[2] or payment for goods supplied in the course of the liquidation without the leave of the Court: (Rule 163). The leave of the Court must be obtained before a proposed transaction is entered into[3] and the costs of so doing must be borne by the person seeking leave: (Rule 164). Any transaction entered into or profit made from such transaction, without the leave of the Court first having been obtained, may be set aside or recovered as the case may be. In one case, for instance, a solicitor was deprived of his costs where he acted for the Liquidator at a time when his managing clerk was on the committee.[4]

Powers of the Committee of Inspection in a Creditors' Voluntary Winding-Up are as follows:

(i) To direct which books shall be kept and inspect them: Rule 172(3).

(ii) To fix the Liquidator's remuneration: s.296(1).

(iii) To authorise the disposal of the books and papers at the conclusion of the Liquidation: s.341(1)(b).

(iv) To sanction the continuance of the Directors' powers: s.296(2).

(v) To sanction the payment of any class of Creditors in full or compromises with Creditors, members or other debtors: s.303(1)(a).

(vi) To decide on investment and realisation of investments of money at the Bank of England: Rule 173.

[1] *Re Bulmer* [1937] 1 All E.R. 323.
[2] *Dowling* v *Lord Advocate* [1963] S.L.T. 146.
[3] *Re Gallard* [1896] 1 Q.B. 68.
[4] *Re F. T. Hawkins & Company Limited* [1952] Ch. 881.

(vii) To sanction the sale of assets in exchange for shares: ss.287 and 298.

Where there is no Committee of Inspection the above powers are generally exercisable by the Creditors as a body, except that in the case of (v) the Creditors *or* the Court can act, (vi) the Liquidator submits a case to the Department of Trade and (vii) the Court exercises the power. In the event of conflict between the views of the Committee and those of the Creditors, the Liquidator should follow the latter, who have the power to remove their nominees by ordinary resolution passed at a meeting of which seven days' notice, stating the object of the meeting, has been given: s.253(6).

(3) *Meetings of Creditors*

(i) *If a Declaration of Solvency* has been filed, there will be no meetings of Creditors during the Winding-Up, except in one situation. This arises when the Liquidator forms the opinion at any time during the Winding-Up that the Company will not be able to pay its debts within the period stated in the declaration.

In this case, the Liquidator must call a meeting of the Creditors forthwith and lay before the meeting a statement of assets and liabilities (s.288). In such circumstances the provisions of ss. 299 and 300 which relate to the holding of meetings of the Company and its Creditors and to dissolution apply as if the Winding-Up were a Creditors' Winding-Up and not a Members' Winding-Up (s.291). Those who made the Declaration of Solvency run the risk of criminal proceedings under s.283(3).

(ii) *In a Creditors' Winding-Up*, if there is a Committee of Inspection, there is no need to call Creditors' meetings for any of the matters within the powers of the Committee (see above, page 59).

(iii) *Certain matters* are *outside the powers of the Committee* and, for these, meetings of the Creditors will have to be held. They include:

(a) Appointing a new Liquidator: s.297.

(b) Receiving the Liquidator's report at the end of the first year and each year thereafter: s.299.

(c) Appointing the Committee of Inspection either at their first meeting under s.293, or at any subsequent meeting: s.295.

(d) Filling up vacancies in the Committee of Inspection: s.253(7).
(e) Receiving the Liquidator's final accounts at the final meetings: s.300.
Liquidators frequently ascertain the wishes of the Creditors on major matters affecting the liquidation: the Liquidator has power to call a meeting of Creditors to ascertain their wishes at any time under Rule 127.

(iv) Where there is *no Committee of Inspection,* meetings of Creditors will also be held for:
(a) Directing which books shall be kept: Rule 172(3).
(b) Fixing the Liquidator's remuneration: s.296(1).
(c) Authorising final disposal of books and papers: s.341(1)(b).
(d) Sanctioning continuance of Directors' powers: s.296(2).
(e) Sanctioning payment of any class of Creditors in full and compromises with Creditors, members or other debtors: s.303(1)(a).

(4) *Procedure for Meetings of Creditors*
The Liquidator can call meetings at any time under Rule 127(2) and will follow the procedure laid down by rules 127–156. The main requirements are as follows:
(a) Seven days' notice in the *London Gazette* and in a local paper: Rule 129.
(b) Seven days written notice by post to every Creditor appearing by the Company's books to be a Creditor (Rule 129), and to any creditor of whom the Liquidator has notice.
(c) The notice should set out the Agenda: see Form 35A on page 179.
(d) The Liquidator or his nominee will be Chairman: Rule 133.
(e) General and special Proxy Forms must be sent out with the notices; the name of the Liquidator or any other person must not be inserted as proxy, in advance: Rule 148.
(f) A creditor can appoint the Liquidator as his proxy, if he wishes: Rule 152, but the Liquidator must not solicit proxies or the Court may disallow his remuneration: Rule 151.

(g) Minutes and a list of those present must be kept and signed: Rule 145. (Form 37 on page 182.)

(h) The right to vote and the value of the debt are as determined by the Chairman (usually the Liquidator): Rule 143. It is not essential in a Voluntary Winding-Up that a formal proof should have been lodged and admitted: Rule 139.

(i) The Chairman's decision as to admission of votes is subject to appeal to the Court, and if in doubt he should allow the Creditor to vote, subject to it being declared invalid if an objection is sustained: Rule 143.

(j) Creditors do not vote on unliquidated, contingent or unascertained debts: Rule 140.
Secured Creditors should only vote in respect of any unsecured balance, and if they vote in respect of the whole sum they are treated as having surrendered their security, unless the Court is satisfied that this was due to inadvertence: Rule 140.

(k) A resolution is passed when approved by a majority in *number and value* of those voting either personally or by proxy: Rule 134. In *re Caston Cushioning Ltd.*[1] there was a majority in value but not in number to nominate a Liquidator, and the appointment was held to be invalid.

(l) A quorum is *three Creditors* in person or by proxy (Rule 138(1)) or all the Creditors, if not more than three. If there is no quorum within half an hour, the meeting is adjourned, usually for one week: Rule 138(2).

(m) The meeting can be adjourned by the Chairman with its consent: Rule 137. (See Form 42 on page 186.)
The Court has a residuary power to order meetings of Creditors or Contributories at any time: s.346. The section provides that the Court may have regard to the rights of the Creditors and contributories as proved to it by sufficient evidence and that in the case of Creditors regard should be had to the value of each Creditor's debt and in the case of contributories to the number of votes conferred on each contributory either under the Companies Act 1948 or by the Articles. The Court will normally follow the wishes of the majority of the Creditors, if reasonable, in the absence of special circumstances.[2]

[1] [1955] 1 W.L.R. 163.

[2] *Re A.B.C. Coupler & Engineering Company Limited* [1961] 1 W.L.R. 243.

CHAPTER 9

Matters Arising in Winding-Up

(1) *Remuneration of Liquidator*

In a *Members' Winding-Up*, the Liquidator's remuneration is fixed by the members, in general meeting, either on his appointment or at any time afterwards (s.285). If the members fail to fix the amount of the Liquidator's remuneration the Court has power to do so.[1]

In a *Creditors' Winding-Up*, the remuneration is fixed by the Committee of Inspection or, if none, by the Creditors in general meeting (s.296(1)). The following points should be borne in mind:

(a) In practice, remuneration is usually fixed by reference to a percentage on realisations and a percentage on distributions (see e.g. Form 26 on page 166).

(b) In fixing his remuneration the Liquidator may be faced with something of a dilemma. If his remuneration is fixed at the commencement of the liquidation without knowledge of all the difficulties which may arise in his administration the Liquidator may find himself undercharging. On the other hand if he waits to the end of the liquidation he may find opposition to his proposed charges.

(c) There is no fixed scale fee for remuneration and what is a proper fee for the Liquidator is a matter for agreement, or, if necessary, for fixing by the Court. When the Court fixes the Liquidator's remuneration it usually has regard to the Official Receiver's scale under The Companies (Department of Trade) Fees Order, 1980[2] and to the hourly rates usually charged by experienced firms of accountants regularly administering liquidations.

(d) Whether or not the Liquidator's remuneration is fixed at the commencement of the liquidation he will normally wish to receive interim payments on account of his remuneration before the liquidation is closed. The Liquidator should be

[1] *Re Carton Limited* (1923) 128 L.T. 629.
[2] S.I. 1980 No. 2008; see p. 187 post.

careful to ensure that he obtains approval for interim payments to be made.

(e) The Liquidator's remuneration is one of the expenses of the liquidation and ranks in priority to the claims of preferential and ordinary unsecured Creditors, (s.309). However, where the assets are not sufficient to pay all the costs, the Court can direct the order in which the costs are to be paid (ss.267, 307), usually by following the order prescribed by Rule 195, which applies to compulsory liquidations.

(f) The Liquidator must not accept any benefits, beyond his proper remuneration, from any solicitor, auctioneer or other person connected with the Company; nor must he share his remuneration with any such persons: Rule 161.

(2) *Removal of Liquidator*

Those who appointed the Liquidator (i.e. members or Creditors) have no power to remove him; only the Court can do this "on cause shown": s.304(2). "Cause shown" implies unfitness in a wide sense,[2] but the Court will exercise its power whenever it is satisfied that it is in the interest of the parties to do so[3], e.g. where the Liquidator is mentally unfit,[4] or where there is a conflict of interest,[5] or where the Liquidator disregards the wishes of the Creditors in an insolvent liquidation[6] or where the Liquidator makes default in the performance of any of his duties.[7]
Having removed a Liquidator under s.304, the Court can appoint a replacement (s.304(2)), but the dismissed Liquidator can appeal against his removal.[8] The application for removal can be made to the Court by any Creditor or contributory.[9]

(3) *Vacancies*

Vacancy in the office of Liquidator can occur by:

(a) *Death or resignation:* No procedure is prescribed for resignation, but the right to do so is implied by sections 286 (members)

[1] *Re Mortimers (London) Limited* [1937] Ch. 289.
[2] *Re Sir John Moore Gold Mining Company* (1879) 12 Ch. D. 325.
[3] *Re Adam Eyton Limited* [1887] 36 Ch. D. 299.
[4] *Re North Molton Mining Company Limited* [1886] 54 L.T. 602.
[5] *Re Charterland Goldfields* (1909) 26 T.L.R. 132.
[6] *Re Rubber & Produce Investment Trust* [1915] 1 Ch. 382.
[7] *Re Ryder Installations* [1966] 1 W.L.R. 524.
[8] *Re Adam Eyton Limited* (1887) 36 Ch. D. 299.
[9] *Re New De Kaap Limited* [1908] 1 Ch. 589.

and 297 (creditors). The Liquidator should call meetings of the members (and Creditors where appropriate) to receive his resignation and appoint a replacement. If they will not agree, he will probably have to apply to the Court under s.304.

(b) *Removal* by the Court under s.304 (see *supra*).

(c) *Deemed removal*, where a Receiving Order in bankruptcy is made against him: Rule 168.

Where a vacancy occurs it may be filled:

(a) in a Members' Winding-Up, subject to any arrangement with the Creditors, by the Company in general meeting: s.286;

(b) in a Creditors' Winding-Up, by the Creditors, except where the previous Liquidator was appointed by or at the direction of the Court: s.297;

(c) in either case by the Court itself: s.304.

The Members' or Creditors' Meetings may be called by any contributory (s.286) or Creditor (Rule 129(3)) as the case may be.

The Court's power applies whenever there is no Liquidator acting (s.304) and also when an additional Liquidator is required.[1]

(4) *Joint Liquidators*

Two or more Liquidators can be appointed in a Voluntary Liquidation, and their powers are then exercised by such one or more of them as is determined at the time of appointment. Failing this, any two can act: s.303(3). The joint Liquidators cannot, themselves, delegate their powers, although they can delegate the execution of a particular document.[2]

They will, therefore, have to agree on any course to be taken. If one dies, the survivors can continue to act if they are two or more: s.303(3). If there is only one survivor, he cannot act alone except for the purpose of calling a meeting to appoint a new joint Liquidator,[3] unless the terms of the appointment empowered the survivor to act alone in such circumstances.

(5) *Change of Registered Office*

The Liquidator may often find it convenient to conduct the Winding-Up from his own offices and for this purpose he may wish to change the Registered Office to that address, so that he receives notice of all communications and proceedings. No resolution is

[1] *Re Sunlight Incandescent Gas Lamp Company* [1900] 2 Ch. 728.

[2] *Re London & Mediterranean Bank* (1868) 3 Ch. App. 651.

[3] *Re Metropolitan Bank and Jones* (1876) 2 Ch. D. 366.

necessary and all that is required is the filing with the Registrar of the usual form of Notice within fourteen days of the change (s.107(2)). A name-plate must be displayed (s.108(a)) and the seal and Registers should be removed to the new office.

(6) *Personal Indemnity*

A Liquidator does not, normally, assume personal liability on contracts[1] provided he clearly contracts as agent for the Company and not in his own capacity.

However, he may wish to obtain a personal indemnity from those appointing him, and he will certainly do so if, at their request, he makes a distribution before all liabilities are ascertained. A specimen form of indemnity is on page 185.

(7) *Solicitors' Costs*

(a) Claims for costs incurred before the commencement of Winding-Up rank as ordinary unsecured debts. However, where the solicitor has a lien on deeds and papers in his possession he may retain such documents which are in his possession before the Winding-Up until he is paid but not those which he acquired afterwards.[2] The solicitor may also get a charging order on funds which he has recovered,[3] but the lien does not extend to the Company's registers,[4] nor to pre-incorporation costs.[5]

If in doubt as to any solicitors' bill, the Liquidator can ask for it to be taxed, or if it is a non-contentious charge, under the Solicitors' Remuneration Order 1972[6] he may require the solicitor to obtain a certificate of fairness from the Law Society.

The costs of the Winding-Up meetings are not expenses of the liquidation and must not be paid in priority to other claims.[7]

(b) *Costs properly incurred in the course of the Winding-Up* are costs of the liquidation and payable in priority to all other claims:

[1] *Stead, Hazel & Co.* v *Cooper* [1933] 1 K.B. 840.
[2] *Re Rapid Road Transit Company* [1909] 1 Ch. 96.
[3] *Re Born* [1902] 2 Ch. 433.
[4] *Re Capital Fire Insurance Association* (1883) 24 Ch. D. 408. C.A.
[5] *Re Gallard* [1885] 31 Ch. D. 296.
[6] S.I. 1972 No. 1139.
[7] *Re J. Russell Electronics Ltd.* [1968] 1 W.L.R. 1252.

s.309. Accordingly, solicitors, accountants, estate agents, auctioneers and other professional advisers acting for the Liquidator are entitled to be paid in full out of the assets of the Company in liquidation.[1] If the assets will not cover all the expenses of liquidation, the costs of professional advisers will rank before the Liquidator's own remuneration.[2] However, if the assets are not sufficient to pay such costs in full the Liquidator will not be personally liable, e.g. to his solicitors, unless he has given a personal undertaking.[3] The Liquidator may be at risk of personal liability if he overpays a solicitor employed by him in the course of the Winding-Up and he may therefore ask the solicitor to undertake to refund any part of his bill which may be disallowed. If a solicitor recovers money on the Liquidator's instructions, he has no lien on it for work done before Winding-Up.[4] The principle that costs of the liquidation are payable out of the assets in priority to all other claims applies generally to all the costs properly incurred in litigation on the Company's behalf,[5] and even if the Liquidator is ordered to pay the costs personally in the proceedings, he will not normally lose his right to indemnity out of the assets so far as assets exist for payment of such costs.[6] If proceedings are taken by the Liquidator in the name of the Company in liquidation, defendants can apply for security for costs under s.447, and the fact that the Company is in liquidation is a prima facie indication that it will be unable to pay such costs.[7] However, where such proceedings are commenced by the Liquidator personally, security for costs will not be ordered. When involved in litigation, the Liquidator should protect his interests by exercising caution, applying for the directions of the Court, where appropriate,[8] consulting the Creditors or contributories,[9] or Committee of Inspection and, in a difficult

[1] See *Re Introductions Limited No. 2* [1969] 1 W.L.R. 1359.

[2] *Re Massey* (1870) L.R. 9 Eq. 367.

[3] *Re Trueman's Estate* (1872) L.R. 14 Eq. 278.

[4] *Allen* v *Montagus & Cox & Cardale* [1934] The Accountant L.R. 15th December 1934.

[5] *Re Wenborn and Company* [1905] 1 Ch. 413.

[6] *Re Wilson Lovatt & Sons Ltd* [1977] 1 All E.R. 274.

[7] *Northampton Coal Co.* v *Midland Waggon Co.* (1878) 7 Ch. D. 500 but see *Sir Lindsay Parkinson & Co Ltd* v *Triplan Ltd* (1973) 1 Q.B. 609 were it was indicated that an order for security for costs was discretionary and that the court was not bound to order security for costs against a company in liquidation, per Lord Denning MR on pp 625–626.

[8] *Re Silver Valley Mines* (1882) 21 Ch. D. 381.

[9] *Re Agricultural Industries Limited* [1952] 1 All E.R. 1188.

case where the assets are not substantial, by asking for an indemnity.[1]

(8) *Registered Land*

If the Company owns land which is registered at H.M. Land Registry, the Liquidator should ensure that the Land Certificate (or Charge Certificate if the mortgagees will agree) is lodged at the Registry with applications for:

(a) An entry of his appointment;

(b) A restriction to the effect that no disposition other than a Transfer on Sale will be registered unless pursuant to powers granted by the Companies Act 1948 or under an order of the Chief Land Registrar: Land Registration Rules 1925, Rule 185. The application should be accompanied by a certificate as to the Declaration of Solvency, if applicable, and certified copies of the resolution(s) appointing him.

(9) *Stamp Duties*

(a) Section 339(1) gives certain exemptions from Stamp Duty in the case of a Creditors' Winding-Up. Every transfer relating solely to property of the Company, which after the execution of the transfer, remains the property of the Company, and every written instrument relating solely to the property of the Company, are exempt from Stamp Duty. The exemption only applies if the stamp duty would have been payable by the Company itself.

(b) Distribution of assets to the members *in specie* attracts only 50p Stamp Duty, but it should be adjudicated: Stamp Act 1891, Sch. 1.

(10) *Liquidators and Receivers*

A liquidator may often find that a Receiver has been appointed by a debenture holder over the assets of the Company prior to liquidation. The relationship between the Liquidator and a Receiver may give rise to difficulty since normally the Receiver is primarily concerned on behalf of a particular Creditor or group of Creditors. The following is a brief summary of general principles which may govern the relationship between the Liquidator and the Receiver.

[1] See e.g. *Re London Metallurgical Company* [1895] 1 Ch. 758.

(a) *Receivership Continues*

The commencement of a Voluntary Liquidation and the appointment of a liquidator does not determine a Receiver's power to deal with, realise or sell the assets of the Company charged under a debenture.[1] If, however, the Receiver has been appointed the agent of the Company under the terms of the debenture, as is commonly the case, his agency terminates on the commencement of the liquidation[2] and thereafter the Receiver acts as a principal with a right of indemnity out of the assets of the Company.[3]

(b) *Receiver's right to the Assets*

If, as is commonly the case, the Receiver is appointed by debenture holders having a floating charge over the whole of the assets and undertaking, the floating charge will crystallise on his appointment.[4] Thus, the Receiver will be effectively entitled to possession of the whole of the assets, and the Liquidator must give them up to him on request.[5] However, the Receiver is not entitled to retain possession of the minute book, share register and other books which relate to the management of the Company.[6] The Liquidator, in turn, is entitled to demand from the Receiver all of the Company's books and documents apart from those which relate to the title of the debenture holders.[7]

(c) *Validity of Receiver's Appointment*

The Liquidator should investigate whether the Receiver has been validly appointed. The Receiver's appointment may be invalid or capable of being set aside where the charge under which he has been appointed is itself invalid, e.g. for non-compliance with s. 95(1), see p 48 *ante*, or under ss.320 or 322, see pp 32 and 49 *ante*. Furthermore, although the charge may be valid the appointment of the Receiver may not have been made in good faith[8] or the requisite formalities not complied with, e.g. where no valid demand as required under the debenture has been made on the Company or where a

[1] *Gosling-Greshall* [1897] A.C. 575: *Gough's Garages* v *Pugsley* [1930] 1 K.B. 615; *Sowman* v *David Samuel Trust Limited* [1978] 1 W.L.R. 22.

[2] *Thomas* v *Todd* [1926] 2 K.B. 511.

[3] See e.g. s.369(2).

[4] *Re Griffin Hotel Company Limited* [1940] 4 All E.R. 324.

[5] *Re Henry Pound, Son & Hutchins* (1889) 42 Ch. D. 402.

[6] *Engel* v *South Metropolitan Brewing Company* [1892] 1 Ch. 442.

[7] Ibid.

[8] *Re Maskelyne British Typewriter Limited* [1898] 1 Ch. 133.

deed of appointment is required and the appointment has simply been made in writing.[1] Where there is such an invalid charge or invalid appointment the Receiver will be a trespasser and liable as such.

(d) *Liquidator as Receiver*

A Receiver may be appointed either by the debenture holders under the terms of their debentures or by the Court in a debenture holders' action[2] or on an originating summons.[3]

It is undesirable for the same person to be both Receiver and Liquidator if there is any possibility of a conflict of interest. Where there is any possibility of conflict the Court may remove the Liquidator, e.g. where the same individual was appointed both Receiver and Liquidator by the shareholders and the unsecured Creditors felt prejudiced by such a dual function.[4] Conversely, in exceptional circumstances it seems that the Court may have power to remove a Receiver and to appoint the Liquidator to act as Receiver also.[5]

(e) *Manager carrying on Business*

The Receiver is usually appointed also as Manager, with power to carry on business for the benefit of the debenture holders. If, after the commencement of the liquidation, the Liquidator feels that the Receiver in carrying on the business of the Company may be jeopardising assets otherwise available for distribution to the unsecured Creditors or shareholders, he may apply to the Court under s.307.

(f) *Misfeasance by Receiver*

The Liquidator has a duty to protect the unsecured creditors and members against any default by the Receiver:

(i) If the Receiver was appointed by the Court, he is an officer of the Court, and interference with him is contempt of Court.[6] Consequently proceedings against him should only be taken with the leave of the Court.[7]

[1] *Windsor Refrigerator Company Limited* v *Branch Nominees Limited* [1961] Ch. 375.

[2] See e.g. *Re Crompton & Company Limited* [1914] 1 Ch. 954.

[3] *Re Francke* (1887) 57 L.J. Ch. 437.

[4] *Re Karamelli & Burnett Ltd* [1917] 1 Ch. 203.

[5] *Perry* v *Oriental Hotels* (1870) L.R. 5 Ch. App. 420; *Bartlett* v *Northumberland Avenue Hotel Co* (1866) 53 L.T. 611. See also *British Linen Co* v *South American and Mexican Co* [1894] 1 Ch. 108; *Re Maskelyne British Typewriter Ltd* (*ante*); *Re Slogger Automatic Co* [1915] 1 Ch. 478.

[6] *Moss S.S. Company* v *Whinney* [1912] A.C. 254 H.L.

[7] See e.g. *L.P. Arthur* (*Insurance*) *Limited* v *Sisson* [1966].

(ii) A Receiver and Manager appointed by the debenture holders is not an "officer of the Company" for the purpose of a *misfeasance summons* under s.333.[1]

(iii) The Company may be able to exercise some control over the Receiver by passing a special resolution for the appointment of an Inspector by the Department of Trade under s.165(a)(1).[2]

(iv) A Receiver whether appointed in, or out, of Court, is personally liable on his contracts except where prior to the liquidation he has expressly excluded his own personal liability. The Receiver has a right of indemnity out of the assets (s.369(2)), but if the Liquidator considers that the Receiver is in default, he may seek to deprive him of the indemnity to the extent of the default[3] and to have his remuneration and expenses disallowed where appropriate.[4]

(v) Although the Receiver's duties are owed primarily to the debenture holders,[5] the Liquidator may be able to hold the Receiver personally liable where the Receiver has not obtained the proper market price for the assets which he has sold.[6]

(vi) If the Receiver defaults in filing any accounts which are required of him (e.g. under s.374) or fails to render proper accounts of his receipts and payments and to pay over to the Liquidator the amount properly payable to him, the Liquidator may apply to the Court by way of summons, to enforce these duties: s.375.

(g) *Preferential Debts*

Where a debenture is secured by a floating charge the Receiver should pay the preferential Creditors in priority to either principal or interest in the debenture. (See s.94(1), where the Receiver is appointed prior to liquidation, and, s.319(5)b, where the Company is in liquidation at the time of the Receiver's appointment.)

(h) *Receiver's Remuneration*

The Liquidator should examine the Receiver's remuneration, which in an appointment in Court will be fixed by the

[1] *Re B. Johnson & Company (Builders) Limited* [1955] Ch. 634.
[2] *R.* v *Board of Trade e.p. St. Martin Preserving Company Limited* [1964] 1 Q.B. 603.
[3] *British Power Traction Company* [1910] 2 Ch. 470.
[4] See e.g. *Re Wood Green Laundry* [1918] 1 Ch. 423.
[5] *Re B. Johnson & Company (Builders) Limited* [1955] Ch. 634.
[6] *Cuckmere Brick Co* v *Mutual Finance Ltd* [1971] Ch. 954.

Court and otherwise in accordance with the terms of the debenture. These may incorporate s.109(6) of the Law of Property Act 1925 which allows a commission of not more than 5% on the gross amount recovered or as fixed by the Court.

In all cases, the Liquidator has the power to apply to the Court to fix the Receiver's remuneration. This power may be exercised notwithstanding that the Receiver has already been paid and where it is so exercised the Receiver may be required to refund any excess of the amount which he has been paid over the amount allowed by the Court, s.371.

(11) *Insolvency in Members' Winding-Up*

(a) In a Members' Winding-Up, the Directors will have made and filed a *Declaration of Solvency* under s.283 to the effect that after full enquiry they have formed the opinion that the Company will be able to pay its debts within, at most, twelve months.[1] This declaration is of the utmost importance as upon it depends the whole course of the liquidation as a Members' Winding-Up. The statement of assets or liabilities contained in the declaration is not required to be checked or verified by any independent source and will be accepted for registration by the Registrar at its face value.

(b) The sanction lies in s.283(3)[2] whereby criminal penalties (two years' imprisonment or a fine or both) are imposed on any Director who makes a declaration "without having reasonable grounds". In any criminal proceedings the Court presumes the Director to be guilty in a case where the debts are not paid within the stated period, unless he can prove himself innocent, i.e. that he had reasonable grounds for his opinion.

(c) Despite these severe penalties, it is quite possible for Directors to err, for example in the realisable value which they put on the assets, and no Director would be acting wisely if he made the declaration in any case where there was the slightest doubt as to the Company's solvency. There should sensibly be a very large margin for error; otherwise only one course is open to the Directors—to call a meeting of Creditors under s.293.

(d) Where the Liquidator forms the opinion that the Company will not be able to pay all its debts within the stated period he

[1] See p. 17 ante.

[2] As amended by the Companies Act 1980.

must forthwith summon a meeting of Creditors and lay before them a statement of assets and liabilities. Failure to do this involves him in liability to criminal proceedings and a fine of one-fifth of the statutory maximum on summary conviction (currently £1000): s.288(2).[1]

(e) Having called a meeting under s.288 the Liquidator must then call annual (s.299) and final (s.300) meetings of Creditors as though the liquidation were a Creditors' Winding-Up. A Liquidator is not, however, required to summon a meeting of Creditors at the end of the first year of the liquidation where the s.288 meeting has been held within three months before the end of that year: s.291.

(12) *Compulsory Order after Voluntary Winding-Up*

Voluntary Winding-Up does not bar the right of any Creditor or contributory to have the Company wound up by the Court (s.310), but the following factors will apply.

(a) Where a *Creditor* petitions as between himself and the Company, he has *the right* to have it compulsorily wound up without having to show that he will be prejudiced.[2]

(b) Where a Creditor petitions as between himself and other Creditors, the majority view will normally prevail unless there are special circumstances.[3] The majority for or against a compulsory order is not however conclusive in itself and the Court has an unfettered discretion to determine what is reasonable in the interests of the general body of Creditors.[4]

(c) Where a petitioning Creditor fails because of the views of the majority, no order as to costs will normally be made,[5] unless he has acted unreasonably.[6]

(d) A *contributory* will have greater difficulty in presenting a successful petition as he must show that the contributories' interests will be prejudiced by the continuation of the Voluntary Winding-Up (s.310). The Court will not want to interfere unless there are circumstances which clearly require investigation.[7]

[1] As amended by the Companies Act 1980.
[2] *Re J. Millward & Company Limited* [1940] Ch. 333.
[3] *Re J. D. Swain Limited* [1965] 1 W.L.R. 909.
[4] *Re Southard & Co Ltd* [1979] 1 W.L.R. 1198.
[5] *Re A.B.C. Coupler & Engineering Company Limited* [1961] 1 W.L.R. 243.
[6] *Re A.E. Hayter & Sons (Porchester) Limited* [1961] 1 W.L.R. 1008.
[7] *Re Haycraft Gold Reduction Company* [1900] 2 Ch. 230.

(e) The Official Receiver has the right to petition under s.224(2) and if he can show that the Voluntary Winding-Up cannot continue with due regard to the interests of the Creditors or contributories the Court will make the order, e.g. where the Liquidator had been convicted of breach of his duties and his appointment had never been confirmed by a Creditors' Meeting.[1]

(f) The Winding-Up *Order* has no effect on the date of commencement of Winding-Up. This still takes effect on the passing of the original resolution: s.229(1). Unless the Court directs otherwise, all steps taken by the voluntary Liquidator are deemed to be valid (s.299(1)), although his remuneration may be reviewed by the Court.[2]

(13) *Stay of Winding-Up*

Under sections 256 and 307 the Court has power to stay a Voluntary Winding-Up. An application for this purpose can be made by the Liquidator or any Creditor or member. The jurisdiction of the Court is discretionary and a stay will not normally be granted unless:

(i) The Creditors have been or will be paid in full or consent to the application;

(ii) The Liquidator's position has been fully safeguarded either by payment of all costs, charges and expenses properly incurred by him, including his remuneration, or by sufficiently securing such payment;

(iii) The Members consent or there is secured to them the right to receive all that they would have received had the Voluntary Winding-Up proceeded to its conclusion.[3]

(14) *Statute-Barred Debts*

Most debts are barred six years after they fall due, unless any acknowledgement or part payment is made in the meantime: (Limitation Act 1939, s.2 and ss. 22–25).[4] Such debts are not liabilities of the Company and the Liquidator must refuse to pay them if the Company is insolvent.[5] Even if the Company is solvent,

[1] *Re Ryder Installations Limited* [1966] 1 W.L.R. 524.
[2] *Re Mortimers (London) Limited* [1937] 2 All E.R. 364.
[3] *Re Calgary and Edmonton Land Co Ltd* [1975] 1 W.L.R. 355.
[4] As amended by the Limitation Amendment Act 1980.
[5] *Re Fleetwood Syndicate* [1915] 1 Ch. 486.

he must also reject the claims unless all the contributories agree to pay them.[1] The inclusion of a debt in a balance sheet may amount to an acknowledgement,[2] and the Liquidator should ensure that he excludes statute-barred debts from any accounts which he prepares.

Time ceases to run on the making of a Winding-Up order, and it is probable that a similar rule applies to a Voluntary Liquidation, so that Creditors may prove, so long as they were not barred at the date of the resolution.[3]

(15) *Compensation for Loss of Office*

The Liquidator may often find that proposals are being made (or have already been carried out) to compensate Directors and staff for their impending loss of employment. He should view them with the greatest care as several factors may be involved;

(a) If the payments are redundancy payments *required by law* or specifically provided for in a service agreement, they are ordinary debts of the Company and no special steps are usually required.

(b) If the *employees* are *not Directors* and have service agreements which will be broken by the termination of their employment, they have a legal claim for compensation which the Liquidator is entitled to settle with them, although he will seek approval if large sums are involved or there are special circumstances.

(c) If the Directors have service agreements which are not invalidated by virtue of the provisions of section 47 of the Companies Act 1980 and which will be broken upon the Winding-Up, such Directors may have a similar legal claim subject, however, to the provisions of s.191. Under s.191 any payment to a Director by way of compensation for loss of office must be disclosed to and approved by the members in general meeting. If the Liquidator finds that any payments have been made without such disclosure and approval he must require the sums to be repaid.[4]
However, s.191 does not apply to a bona fide payment of damages for breach of contract or by way of pension for past services: s.194(3).

[1] *Re Art Reproduction Company Limited* [1952] Ch. 89.

[2] *Jones* v *Bellgrove Properties Limited* [1949] 2 All E.R. 198 C.A.; *Re Gee & Co (Woolwich) Ltd* [1975] Ch. 52; *Re Compania de Electricidad de la Provincia de Buenos Aires Ltd* [1980] Ch. 146.

[3] *Re Fleetwood Syndicate* [1915] 1 Ch. 486.

[4] *Re Duomatic Limited* [1969] 2 Ch. 365 (unless approval has been validly given by the members informally).

(16) *Gratuitous Payments to Employees*

Under s.74(3) of the Companies Act 1980, where a Company has before the commencement of its Winding-Up decided to make a payment for the benefit of persons employed or formerly employed by the Company or any subsidiary in connection with the cessation or transfer of the whole or any part of the undertaking of the Company or any subsidiary, the Liquidator may make the payment out of the assets of the Company available to the members on its Winding-Up. Under s.74(5) of the Companies Act 1980, the power of the Company to make any such payment may be exercised by the Liquidator and the payments made out of the assets of the Company available to the members on its Winding-Up after the Company's liabilities have been fully satisfied and provision made for the costs of the Winding-Up if by ordinary resolution of the members the Liquidator is authorised so to act.

(17) *Compromises, Arrangements and Reconstruction*

(a) *Compromises out of Court*
If a Liquidator wishes to make compromises of any kind, with members, Creditors or debtors, he requires:
  (i) An extraordinary resolution in a Members' Winding-Up; and
  (ii) In a Creditors' Winding-Up, the sanction of the Court, or the Committee of Inspection, or if none, the Creditors: s.245(1) and s.303(1)(a).
The Liquidator cannot therefore enter into a compromise on his own authority, although if he does so, and the other party is not aware of the irregularity, it will be binding on him, and probably on the Company.[1]

(b) *Schemes of Arrangement under s.306*
Where an arrangement with Creditors has been approved by an extraordinary resolution of the Company and three-quarters in number and value of the Creditors, s.306 provides that it will be binding on the Company and its Creditors (s.306(1)), although any Creditor or contributory may, within three weeks from the completion of the arrangement, appeal to the Court which may amend or confirm the arrangement: s.306(2).

(c) *Scheme of Arrangement under s.206*
Where under s.206 a compromise or arrangement is proposed

[1] See *Cyclemakers' Co-operative Supply Company* v *Sims* [1903] 1 K.B. 477.

between the Company and its Creditors or members the consent of the Court must be obtained. The application to the Court for its consent may be made by either the Liquidator or by any Creditor or contributory.

Briefly, the procedure is as follows:

(i) The application is made to the Court by originating summons, to call *meetings* of all the parties concerned.

(ii) At the meetings, a *majority in number*, representing *three-quarters in value* of those Creditors or members (as the case may be) present and voting either in person or by proxy, must approve the Scheme.

(iii) After the meetings have been held a petition is presented to the Court to sanction the Scheme.

If all these steps are successfully taken the Scheme will be binding on all Creditors, members or classes of Creditors or members who are affected, and on the Company and the Liquidator himself. The Court will require to be satisfied that particulars and a full explanation of the Scheme have been given to all parties concerned (s.207), but the Court has the widest possible discretion, and the extent of the disclosure will depend on the circumstances.[1]

Where a scheme is approved, the Court has wide powers to effect the transfer of assets, to allocate to the members shares in a transferee company, and to dissolve the old company without Winding-Up: s.208.

In *Re Trix Limited*[2] it was held that the proper way to distribute the assets of a company other than strictly in accordance with Creditors' rights is by a scheme of arrangement under s.206 which binds all Creditors and not by an agreement or compromise under s.245 which deprives non-assenting Creditors of the Court's protection and prevents them from expressing their views.

(d) *Voluntary Winding-Up and Sale under s.287*

This is the procedure designed for a company which goes into a Members' Winding-Up for the purpose of amalgamation or reconstruction. The Liquidator sells the assets to another Company and, in return, receives shares in that Company, which he distributes amongst the members.

It may also be appropriate where new capital is needed and part of the membership is unwilling to subscribe. By this

[1] See e.g. *Re National Bank Limited* [1966] 1 W.L.R. 819.

[2] [1970] 1 W.L.R. 1421.

procedure partly paid shares in the new Company can be allotted and the dissentient members can either sell their shares to the Liquidator or accept the liability to contribute. The consent of the Court is not required and the procedure is:

(i) *A Special resolution* is passed authorising the Liquidator to receive in consideration for the assets, shares policies or other assets in the new Company for distribution among the members: s.287(1).

(ii) The arrangement is *binding* on the members: s.287(2).

(iii) Any member who did not vote for the resolution may give notice of his *dissent* to the Liquidator *within seven days*, requiring him to either (a) abandon the scheme or (b) buy his interest at a price to be agreed or fixed by arbitration: s.287(3).

(iv) If the Liquidator buys the member's interest he must do so before the Company is dissolved and raise the money in such manner as is determined by special resolution: s.287(4).

(v) If a *Winding-Up or Supervision Order* is made *within one year*, the resolution becomes *void*, unless sanctioned by the Court: s.287(5)

The Court cannot give its consent until the order has been made.[1] Accordingly until twelve months have expired from the passing of the special resolution or the consent of the Court obtained following the making of a Winding-Up order or supervision order within that period there is no certainty that the Scheme will not be invalidated.

Section 287 does not apply to a Creditors' Winding-Up but is extended to it by s.298 save that the powers of the Liquidator under the section cannot be exercised except with the sanction of the Court or of the Committee of Inspection.

(18) *Taxation*

The Liquidator may be confronted with claims for taxation of several types. Some of the more important are the following:

(a) *Corporation Tax*, in respect of the accounting period which will end with the passing of the Winding-Up resolution and outstanding arrears in respect of earlier accounting periods, and in respect of subsequent twelve months' periods commencing on the date of the passing of the Winding-Up

[1] *Re Callao Bis Company* (1889) 42 Ch. D. 169.

resolutions, and a final period up to the completion of Winding-Up: Income and Corporation Taxes Act 1970, s.247.

(b) *Capital Gains*, which are of course excluded from Capital Gains Tax, but included in the profits for Corporation Tax purposes: Income and Corporation Taxes Act 1970, s.265.

(c) *Income Tax* under Schedule F on dividends and distributions: Income and Corporation Taxes Act 1970, s.232.

(d) *Income Tax on Short-fall in distributions*: Finance Act 1972, s.94 and Schedule 16. These provisions continue to apply as if the Company were not being wound up.

(e) *Income Tax* deducted under P.A.Y.E. from earnings of employees, including, where appropriate, Directors: Income and Corporation Taxes Act 1970, s.204.

(f) *Development Land Tax* charged on the realised development value accruing on the disposal of interests in land: Development Land Tax Act 1976, s.1.

(g) Where applicable, *Value Added Tax and Betting and Gaming Duties.*

Except where these claims are preferential under s.319, the Revenue rank with the ordinary Creditors, but the Liquidator will seek clearances whenever a claim is a possibility and he will not distribute until he has such clearances or adequate retentions.

CHAPTER 10

Payment of Debts

Before making any distribution to the members out of the assets which he has realised or taken into his custody a prudent Liquidator should discharge all claims properly made against the Company in liquidation. Of course, if the Company is insolvent no question of distributions to members will arise and by virtue of s.317 the bankruptcy rules as to payment of debts will apply. If there is, therefore, the slightest chance that the Company will turn out to be insolvent a prudent Liquidator will observe the bankruptcy rules.

Where the Liquidator follows the bankruptcy rules the assets will be applied in the payment of claims in the following order:

(1) *Costs charges* and *expenses* properly incurred in the Winding-Up, including the *remuneration* of the Liquidator: s.309.

(2) *Preferential Debts:* s.319.

(3) *Floating Charges:* s.319(5)(b).

(4) *Ordinary Creditors.*

(5) *Deferred Creditors:* s.212(1)(g).

Secured Creditors can, of course, pay themselves out of their security, or rank as ordinary Creditors to the extent that they do not.

(1) The costs and expenses of liquidation are to be paid before all other claims including preferential Creditors: s.309.

(a) In *Re A.B.C. Coupler & Engineering Company Limited No. 3*[1] a landlord argued that rent and other liabilities were liquidation expenses and therefore payable in full. Plowman J held that rent accrued due before the Winding-Up could not be a liquidation expense but that rent accrued due after the Winding-Up could be such an expense. Damages for the breach of repairing covenants which were provable similarly were not a liquidation expense. The true test whether a Liquidator is liable for payment in full of rent accrued due since the commencement of the liquidation is whether the

[1] [1980] 1 W.L.R. 96.

Liquidator retained possession of the property "for the convenience of the winding-up."[1]

(b) The Liquidator's remuneration which forms part of the costs of liquidation is discussed in Chapter 9 above. Such remuneration ranks equally with the other costs and expenses so far as s.309 is concerned, but if the assets are insufficient to pay them all, the Court will have to decide the order of payment under s.267 and is likely to follow the order prescribed for compulsory liquidations by Rule 195, in which the Liquidator's remuneration comes almost at the end of the list. In *Re Mesco Properties Limited*[2] properties were sold at a profit and as a result the Company became liable to Corporation Tax. The Liquidator had a balance in hand which was less than the amount of the Corporation Tax, his remuneration as Liquidator remaining unpaid. The Court held that although the Corporation Tax was not a fee or expense incurred in realising the assets, it arose as a consequence of the sale of assets of the Company and was payable in priority to the other costs and expenses of the liquidation including the Liquidator's remuneration.

(c) If there is a real danger of the assets being insufficient to pay the expenses, the Liquidator may therefore be advised to follow (so far as appropriate) the list set out in Rule 195 which is as follows:

  (i) Fees and expenses properly incurred in preserving, realising or getting in the assets.
  (ii) Taxed costs of the petition.
  (iii) Remuneration of special manager.
  (iv) Cost of making statement of affairs.
  (v) Costs of shorthand-writers for taking examinations.
  (vi) Liquidator's other necessary disbursements.
  (vii) Costs of any person properly employed by the Liquidator.
  (vii) Liquidator's remuneration.
  (ix) Actual out-of-pocket expenses of Committee of Inspection.

(d) Notwithstanding the order of payment set out in Rule 195, a Liquidator may be allowed to keep remuneration paid at a time when he had no reason to think that the assets would be insufficient.[3]

[1] Ibid per Plowman J. at p. 109; see also *Re Downer Enterprises Ltd.* [1974] 1 W.L.R. 1460.

[2] [1980] 1 W.L.R. 96.

[3] See *Re Beni-Felkai Mining Company Limited* [1934] Ch. 406.

(e) In *Re Mawcon Limited,*[1] expenses incurred by the directors as special managers in carrying on the business of the Company for the benefit of the Winding-Up were held to be liquidation expenses. In *Re Introductions Ltd* (*No. 2*)[2] the only available assets were funds obtained by the Company in the course of *ultra vires* trading. Stamp J held that the Liquidator was entitled to pay out of such funds (i) accountants' charges for the preparation of the statement of affairs and (ii) his own costs and charges, on the basis that "a labourer is worthy of his hire". Similarly in *Re Barleycorn Enterprises Limited,*[3] chartered accountants had prepared a statement of affairs after a winding-up order and the Official Receiver had sanctioned a fee to them of £202.50. The assets were insufficient to pay the preferential claims and debenture holders who had a floating charge. The Court of Appeal held that the accountants' fees were payable in priority to both.

(2) The claims of Preferential Creditors rank in priority after the costs of liquidation and before the claims of holders of floating charges (s.319(5)(b)), save where a floating charge has already crystallised *before* the commencement of Winding-Up.[4] Where a floating charge has already crystallised before the commencement of the Winding-Up the provisions of s.94 require payment to preferential Creditors at the date of the appointment of the Receiver or of possession of the assets comprised in the charge being taken by the debenture holder.

The list of preferential creditors is set out in s.319 (as amended) and is as follows:

(a) *Local rates* due at the date of the passing of the resolution for Voluntary Winding-Up which became due within the twelve months prior to that date.[5] The whole amount falling due is preferential even though covering a period after the Winding-Up.[6]

(b) *Income tax,* corporation tax, and any other assessed *taxes, assessed* up to the April 5th preceding the commencement of the Winding-Up and not exceeding any one year's assessment in respect of any one tax (s.319(1)(a)(ii)). The Revenue can select whichever year they wish, where more than one year is unpaid,[7] and different years for different taxes.[8] P.A.Y.E.

[1] [1969] 1 W.L.R. 78. [2] [1969] 1 W.L.R. 1359. [3] [1970] Ch. 465.
[4] *Re Griffin Hotel Company Limited* [1941] Ch. 129.
[5] See Re Piccadilly Estate Hotels Ltd. (1978) 77 L.G.R. 79.
[6] *Re Mannesmann Tube Company Limited* [1901] 2 Ch. 93.
[7] *Re Pratt, I.R.C.* v *Phillips* [1951] Ch. 225.
[8] *Lord Advocate* v *Kelman* (1957) 51 R. & I. T. 177.

deductions for twelve months before commencement of Winding-Up are made preferential by the Finance Act 1952, s.30(2), and these now include deductions from payments to subcontractors under the Finance Act 1971, s.29(6). Similarly Capital Gains Tax is made preferential by virtue of Schedule 10 Paragraph 15 of the Finance Act 1965, Development Land Tax by virtue of s. 42 of the Development Land Tax Act 1976 and Value Added Tax by virtue of s.41 of the Finance Act 1972. Class 4 contributions so far as owed to the Commissioners of Inland Revenue are also preferential (s.153 Social Security Act 1974), as are general betting duty, gaming licence duty and bingo duty under the Betting and Gaming Duties Act 1972 and car tax under Schedule 7 Paragraph 18 of the Finance Act 1972.

Where a Company is appointed representative member of a group of companies for VAT purposes under s.21 of the Finance Act 1972, as any tax due from the representative member is due also from all the other members of the group, s.41 of the Finance Act 1972 renders the tax due capable of being preferential on the liquidation of any of the other Companies within the group.[1]

(c) Wages or salary of any clerk or servant in respect of services rendered to the Company during the four months prior to the commencement of the Winding-Up and all wages of any workman or labourer in respect of services so rendered, not exceeding £800 (s.319(1)(b)).

For this purpose wages include guarantee payments, remuneration on suspension on medical grounds, payments for time off, and remuneration under a protective award due to an employee in accordance with the provisions of the Employment Protection (Consolidation) Act 1978.[2] There must be a contract of service with the Company. Sums due to independent contractors, e.g. labour only subcontractors, are not preferential.[3] A managing director is not it would seem a clerk or servant[4] but a company secretary may be.[5]

(d) Any sum ordered under the Reinstatement in Civil Employment Act 1944 to be paid by way of compensation where the default by reason of which the order for compensation was

[1] *Re Nadler Enterprises Ltd.* [1980] 3 All E.R. 350.
[2] Cf. s. 121 Employment Protection (Consolidation) Act 1978.
[3] *Re C. W. & A. L. Hughes Limited* [1966] 1 W.L.R. 1369.
[4] *Re Newspaper Proprietory Syndicate Limited* [1900] 2 Ch. 349.
[5] *Cairney* v *Back* [1906] 2 K.B. 746.

made occurred before the commencement of the Winding-Up, not exceeding £800, s.319(1)(c)).

(e) Accrued holiday remuneration due to any clerk, servant, workman or labourer on the termination of his employment before or by the effect of the Winding-Up resolution, s.319(1)d; this includes any holiday he would have had if his employment had continued, s.319(1)(b)).

(f) All debts specified in s.93(2) of the Social Security Act 1973 and in s.153(2) of the Social Security Act 1975[1]—these include Class 1 and Class 2 contributions in the period of twelve months immediately preceding the commencement of the Winding-Up.

(g) All amounts due from the Company under the Workmen's Compensation Act 1925 which have accrued before the commencement of the Winding-Up in satisfaction of a right which has arisen in respect of employment before 5th July 1948 or due from the Company under s.3(5) of the Workmen's Compensation (Coal Mines) Act 1934 to an insurer in respect of a liability for satisfaction of a right under the 1925 Act.

(h) *Lenders of money* for the purpose of paying classes (c) and (e) (wages and holiday pay) which has been so paid, stand in the shoes of the employees concerned, i.e. they are *subrogated* to the employees' rights of preference (s.319(4)).

This latter provision tends to be widely construed by the Courts. It has been held sufficient if the arrangement to advance the money is made with wages in mind.[2] However, the normal procedure adopted by Companies and their Banks is to make advances to pay wages on a special wages account. This clearly gives the Bank subrogated rights of preference.[3] A bank has a further advantage in such circumstances if it has a security which is not sufficient to cover the total overdraft. It has been held that the Bank can apply the proceeds of the security first in reducing the non-preferential debt, thereby leaving intact its full preferential rights in respect of the wages advanced.[4]

Those who establish priority under the provisions of s.319 rank *pari passu*, s.319(5). The Crown, as such, has no claim to priority,[5]

[1] If the Company is being wound up voluntarily merely for the purposes of reconstruction or amalgamation with another Company these debts are not preferential.

[2] *Re Rampgill Mill Limited* [1967] 1 Ch. 1138; see also *Re Primrose (Builders) Ltd.* [1950] Ch. 561.

[3] *Re James R. Rutherford & Sons Limited* [1964] 1 W.L.R. 1211; see also *Re E. J. Morel (1934) Ltd.* [1962] Ch. 21.

[4] *Re William Hall (Contractors) Limited* [1967] 1 W.L.R. 948.

[5] *Food Controller* v *Cork* [1923] A.C. 647.

though under s.125 of the Employment Protection (Consolidation) Act 1978 the Secretary of State is entitled to be subrogated to the rights of employees including preferential rights in respect of certain payments made by the Secretary of State to such employees out of the Redundancy Fund.

(3) Ordinary Creditors rank *pari passu* after all preferential debts have been paid, but before paying any class of Creditors in full, the Liquidator requires:

(a) in a member's Winding-Up, an extraordinary resolution of the Company, s.303(1)(a); or

(b) in a creditors' Winding-Up the sanction of the Committee of Inspection or (if none) of a meeting of Creditors or of the Court, s.303(1)(a).

If the Liquidator is at any time in a position to pay something on account to the Creditors, he is entitled to do so and need not wait until his administration is concluded. He is not bound by Rules 119–120 which apply to compulsory liquidations, but may find it convenient to use the Notice of Dividend provided in Form 65 (see page 177).

c *(4) Postponed claims*, which are postponed until all the ordinary Creditors have been paid, comprise:

(a) Where the Company is insolvent claims to outstanding interest exceeding a rate of 5% per annum on debts which have been proved (s.66 Bankruptcy Act 1914).[1]

(b) Sums due to a member "in his capacity as a member", whether by way of dividends, profits or otherwise. Such sums are not allowed to compete with the debts of other Creditors (s.212(1)(g)). This section does not affect sums which are due to a member in some other capacity, e.g. as a lender. These rank equally with the other ordinary Creditors.
The deferment of dividends under this section applies equally to former shareholders.[2]

(c) Where the Company is or becomes solvent those debts which are not provable where the Company is insolvent become provable because in such circumstances the provisions of s.317 are replaced by those of s.316. However, even where the Company is solvent the Liquidator is not required to pay (i) statute-barred debts[3] or (ii) tax claims by a foreign state.[4]

[1] See p. 52 *ante*.
[2] *Re Consolidated Gold Fields of New Zealand Limited* [1953] Ch. 689.
[3] *Re Fleetwood Light Syndicate* [1915] 1 Ch. 486.
[4] *Government of India* v *Taylor* [1955] A.C. 491.

CHAPTER 11

Rights of Members

In a Winding-Up the members have two main concerns: Will they have to contribute? Will they participate in any surplus?

Contributions

(1) Every person who is or has been a member of a Company within the twelve months immediately prior to the commencement of the Winding-Up thereof is liable to contribute to the assets of the Company and is a "contributory" within the meaning of s.213. The definition of "contributory" therefore includes the holders of fully paid up shares, but since the liability of any contributory is limited to the amount remaining unpaid on the shares in respect of which he is liable, holders of fully paid up shares are not required to contribute further (see s.212).

Partly paid shares are uncommon in practice, because they are unpopular both with companies and their members—with companies because of the difficulty of recovering calls, and with members because they have a contingent liability to pay at some uncertain date which will never be known until a call is made.

(2) There are perhaps three circumstances in which the question of contributions is likely to arise in practice:

(a) *Unlimited companies,* whose members are each fully liable for all the debts, with rights of contribution from one another. Section 212(1).

(b) Some companies adopt the procedure of issuing partly paid shares to their executives as an alternative to options. Thus the executive might take up one-pound shares on the basis that 1p is paid on allotment and the balance of 99p in, say, four years' time. In a rising market, this gives the holder the same benefits as an option although imposing on him a legal obligation to pay. In such a case, the Liquidator can call up the whole balance, even though the date for payment has not arrived.[1]

[1] *Re Cordova Union Gold Company* [1891] 2 Ch. 580.

(c) Shares credited as fully paid may prove, on examination by the Liquidator, to have been credited wrongly. If so, the shares remain unpaid to the extent of the excess, which can then be called up. The Liquidator will be most likely to encounter this situation where shares have been allotted for a consideration other than cash. This fact will be apparent to him from the contract or memorandum which will have been filed under s.52.

The general principle is that the adequacy of the consideration cannot usually be enquired into, e.g. where a business is sold to the Company for a price which is excessive.[1] The Court will not enquire into the adequacy of the consideration, unless there is *fraud,* or the consideration is *illusory,* or the contract shows, on the face of it, that the consideration must have been inadequate. Thus in *Hong Kong and China Gas Company Limited* v *Glen*[2] in return for a concession, the Company agreed to allot to Glen, as fully paid, one-fifth of any increase in the share capital. It was held that the allotments must be made, but Glen would have to pay for them because as the Company's obligation extended indefinitely and for an indefinite amount it could not relate to the value of the property transferred by Glen.

Even shares credited as paid in cash may be open to attack by the Liquidator who will want to see that cash has actually been received by the Company. An allotment is properly made for cash, if in consideration of a debt immediately payable,[3] but not under any other circumstances. There must be on the Company's side a bona fide debt payable at once, e.g. for the purchase of property, and on the member's side a bona fide liability to pay at once for the shares.[4] A promise of future services is not present consideration for an allotment,[5] although the Company could have agreed to pay immediately for the services and applied that money in paying up the shares.[6]

(3) If, after consideration of the above matters, the Liquidator finds that any members are liable to contribute and that such contributions will be required he will settle lists of contributories, for

[1] *Re Wragg Limited* [1879] 1 Ch. 796.
[2] [1914] 1 Ch. 527.
[3] *Spargo's Case* (1873) L.R. 8 Ch. App. 407.
[4] *Larocque* v *Beauchemin* [1897] A.C. 358.
[5] *Re Richmond Hotel Company* (1867) 2 Ch. App. 527.
[6] *Gardner* v *Iredale* [1912] 1 Ch. 700.

which he has the powers conferred on the Court, and which are prima facie evidence of liability (s.303(1)(c)). He will settle two lists:

(a) An "A" list of members at the date of Winding-Up, who are primarily liable.

(b) A "B" list of those who ceased to be members within the last twelve months and whose liability is limited to any deficiency on the "A" list contributions, in respect of debts incurred while they were members, after applying all assets and contributions *pari passu* towards all the debts: s.212(1)(a)(b)(c).

(4) Having settled the Lists, the Liquidator can proceed to make his calls. In this respect also, he is given the powers conferred on the Court by s.303(1)(d), and he can exercise the power to make calls not only for the purpose of paying the debts and the costs of liquidation, but also for adjusting the rights of the members amongst themselves.[1] Thus it is not necessary for the Liquidator to show that there will be debts outstanding before he can make a call.

The Liquidator should normally record the making of the calls by signing a document to that effect and giving notice to the contributories. (Form 43 on page 186). In fixing the amount of the call, he may take into account the probability that some of the contributories may default (s.260(2)). Any dispute or failure to pay can be dealt with by application under s.307, by way of summons, in which all defaulting contributories can be dealt with together (a "Balance Order"): Rule 90. Alternatively the Liquidator can sue for the recovery of the call in the ordinary way as, once made, the call becomes a speciality debt, i.e. with a twelve-year limitation period: s.214.

Set-off is not normally allowed to a contributory against calls,[2] at least, until all the Creditors have been paid in full (s.259(3)). Set-off arising from independent dealings, otherwise than in his capacity as a member, may be allowed to a contributory of an unlimited company: s.259(2). To make any *compromises* in respect of calls, the Liquidator must get the sanction of the appropriate body under s.303(1)(a).

Distributions to Members

The second stage at which the members have a financial interest in a Liquidation is in the distribution of the surplus assets, when all

[1] *Welton* v *Saffery* [1897] A.C. 299.
[2] *Re Rhodesia Goldfields Limited* [1910] 1 Ch. 239.

Creditors and the costs of Liquidation, have been paid. Until this point is reached, members have no claims.[1] The Liquidator must distribute such surplus among them "according to their rights and interest in the Company" except in so far as the Articles otherwise provide (s.302). The Liquidator will, therefore, look at the Articles and follow them, although an outright prohibition against return of capital to the members will be invalid.[2] Subject thereto the procedure will be as follows:

(1) First, the position of the members is *adjusted,* if necessary, so that their contributions of capital are equal. This can be done, either by making calls on those who have paid less than others, or by notional entries, treating the calls as having been paid and then deducting them from the sums to be returned to the members concerned.[3] Any discounts which have been wrongly allowed can be disposed of in this way.[4]

(2) *Paid-up capital is then returned* pro rata if all the shares rank equally. If there are different classes, the Articles or terms of issue may give priority to some. Unless preference as to return of capital is expressly given, it will not normally be implied.[5] Arrears of preference dividend are similarly not payable on Winding-Up, unless they have been declared, or are conferred expressly or by necessary implication, by the Articles[6] (in which case they would be paid gross unless the Articles require the notional tax to be deducted). Nor are Premiums paid on shares repayable, unless the Articles require it.[7]

(3) *Any balance will then be distributed* to the members in proportion to the holdings of nominal capital.[8] The fact that part of the surplus may represent undistributed profits is irrelevant.[9]

(4) Where there is more than one class of shares their rights will depend on the Articles, but prima facie rights given are exhaustive, so that if shares are preferential as to dividend or return of capital, they will not be entitled to participate in any surplus.[10] The burden is thus on the preference shareholders to show, by clear inference or

[1] *Elkins* v *Capital Guarantee Society* [1900] 16 T.L.R. 423.

[2] *Re Merchant Navy Supply Association* [1947] 1 All E.R. 894.

[3] *Re Syston & Thurmaston Gas Light & Coke Company Limited* [1937] 2 All E.R. 322.

[4] *Re Weymouth Steam Packet Company* [1891] 1 Ch. 66.

[5] *Welton* v *Saffery* [1897] A.C. 299.

[6] *Re Catalinas Warehouses and Mole Ltd.* [1947] 1 All E.R. 51.

[7] *Ibid.*

[8] *Re Driffield Gas Light Company* [1898] 1 Ch. 451.

[9] *Re Accrington Steam Tramways Company* [1909] 2 Ch. 40.

[10] *Prudential Assurance Company Limited* v *Chatterley-Whitfield Collieries Company Limited* [1949] A.C. 512.

express terms, that they are entitled to share in any surplus.[1] They failed to discharge this burden in *Re Saltdean Estate Company Limited*[2] where the Articles gave them the right to participate in profits while the Company was a going concern, but to receive their paid up capital only on liquidation.

(5) These rules must always be construed in the light of the Memorandum and Articles and the terms of issue of the shares concerned. Table A contains no provisions as to return of capital, leaving the Company free to issue shares on such terms as to "return of capital" or otherwise as the Company may from time to time by ordinary resolution determine: Article 3.

If the Articles use the expression "surplus assets", it must be construed in the light of the surrounding circumstances, as to whether it means (a) surplus after payment of debts[3] or (b) surplus after return of capital.[4]

(6) One provision on this subject which the Articles are likely to contain is power for the Liquidator, with the sanction of an extraordinary resolution of the Company, to divide the whole or part of the assets *in specie* among the members. For this purpose, he will usually be given power to set such value as he deems fair upon the property and to determine how the division shall be carried out: Table A, Article 135. This power is often useful in a Members' Winding-Up, and even if not contained originally in the Articles, it can be inserted by special resolution and then exercised. A transfer or conveyance will be executed by the Company in the usual way, with the attestation of the Liquidator and, in practice, *ad valorem* 1% stamp duty is not charged, a 50p stamp being accepted. This concession does not extend to a company which is a going concern.[5] A specimen form of resolution to sanction such a distribution is on page 185.

(7) The Liquidator may reach a stage when he has got in a substantial proportion of the assets and has fully ascertained the extent of the liabilities. In such circumstances the Liquidator may make a distribution on account to members provided that he retains sufficient to cover the amount of the liabilities and of the costs of the liquidation including his remuneration. Although an overpayment can be recovered from the contributories,[6] a Liquidator may be

[1] *Re Isle of Thanet Electricity Supply Company Limited* [1950] Ch. 161.
[2] [1968] 1 W.L.R. 1844.
[3] *Dimbula Valley (Ceylon) Tea Company Limited* v *Laurie* [1961] Ch. 353.
[4] *Re Ramel Syndicate Limited* [1911] 1 Ch. 749.
[5] *Associated British Engineering Ltd.* v *I.R.C.* [1940] 4 All E.R. 278.
[6] *Re Birkbeck Permanent Benefit Building Society* [1915] 1 Ch. 400.

personally liable to pay an outstanding Creditor where he has had funds in hand which he has distributed to contributories.[1] There is no provision in a Voluntary Winding-Up for a Liquidator to obtain a release (in a Compulsory Winding-Up he can apply to the Department of Trade under s.251), but where he is being requested to make interim payments, there is nothing to prevent him asking the members to sign a release and an idemnity against personal liability.

(8) Any *unclaimed or undistributed assets* which have been in the Liquidator's hands for six months must be paid into the Insolvency Services Account at the Bank of England (s.343), as must any such assets which are still in his hands at the date of dissolution: (Rule 199(3)). The sums to be paid in under s.343 are ascertained by reference to the six-monthly statements provided by the Liquidator, under Rule 197, and the Department of Trade may allow the Liquidator to retain sufficient for the immediate purposes of the Liquidation: (Rule 199(2)). Sums paid in under these provisions may be paid out either on application by the persons entitled, supported by a certificate from the Liquidator (s.343(3), Rule 203), or on application by the Liquidator so that he may distribute them himself (Rule 204). Applications are made to the Department of Trade, which can require accounts and particulars from the Liquidator at any time: Rules 200, 201.

[1] *Pulsford* v *Devenish* [1903] 2 Ch. 625.

CHAPTER 12

Completion of Winding-Up

As soon as the affairs of the Company are fully wound up so far as the Liquidator is aware[1], the Liquidator can proceed to the dissolution of the Company. The steps to be taken are as follows:

(1) *Final Account*

He will prepare an account, showing how the Winding-Up has been conducted and the property of the Company disposed of: see s.290(1) in the case of a Members' Winding-Up and s.300(1) in the case of a Creditors' Winding-Up. The account should be on Form 110, Rule 182 (see pages 161 and 166).

(2) *Final Meetings*

In a Members' Winding-Up he will then summon the *Final Meeting* of the Company to which the account will be presented (s.290(1)). In a Creditors' Winding-Up he will also summon a Final Meeting of the Creditors for the same purpose, and to follow immediately afterwards: s.300(1).

(3) *Notices*

The meetings are called by advertisement in the *Gazette,* at least one month beforehand (s.290(2), s.300(2)). The Act and Rules do not specifically require individual notices to the members and Creditors, although the members are probably entitled to notice under the Articles (Table A, Article 50), as the meeting will be a general meeting of the Company. In practice, the Liquidator will normally give notice to every member and Creditor at the same time as he publishes the advertisement in the *Gazette,* so that all parties will have one month's notice. (Specimens on pages 165 and 169.)

[1] *Re Cornish Manures Ltd.* [1967] 1 W.L.R. 807.

(4) *Agenda*

The only essential business is to receive the Liquidator's Final Account and his explanation thereof: cf. s.290(1), s.300(1). It is not essential that there should be a resolution approving the account, but the Liquidator should normally ask for such a resolution, particularly as this will also provide him with formal approval of his own remuneration and expenses and of the distributions which he has made. He or his nominee will be Chairman: Rule 133. Irrespective of whether a resolution is passed the Liquidator must still file his returns (see below). It is open to any person interested to apply to the Court for the dissolution to be deferred: s.290(4), s.300(4).

(5) *Disposal of Books and Papers*

Another matter which is commonly dealt with at the Final Meetings is the disposal of books and papers. In a Members' Winding-Up, the members can by an extraordinary resolution direct their disposal, but in a Creditor's Winding-Up, the power rests with the Committee of Inspection, s.341(1). If there is no Committee, the Creditors can direct the disposal, by ordinary resolution, at their final meeting: (s.341(1)). In any event, the Liquidator's responsibility for books and papers will cease five years from dissolution (s.341(2)), though the Department of Trade may make orders preventing disposal within the five-year period (Rule 206). If the extraordinary resolution is passed by the members, it must be filed within fifteen days and the terms of the resolution must be set out verbatim in the notice (s.143). (Specimen form of resolution on page 171).

(6) *Remuneration*

The next matter which the Liquidator may wish to deal with at the Final Meetings is his own remuneration, if not already approved. In a *Members' Winding-Up,* this may be fixed by the members in general meeting, either on his appointment or at any other meeting (s.285). The remuneration is shown on his Final Account (Form 110)[1] and the Final Meeting is an appropriate time at which to secure an ordinary resolution approving it, although approval of the account, will, in itself, constitute such approval. Where the Company does not approve any remuneration, the Court can do so.[2]

[1] Specimen at p. 161.
[2] *Re Carton Limited* (1923) 128 L.T. 629.

In a *Creditors' Winding-Up* the Liquidator must have his remuneration approved by the Committee of Inspection. If there is no Committee, the approval rests with the Creditors (s.296(1)), and it may, again, be convenient to get this approval at their Final Meeting.

Where a Compulsory Order Winding-Up is made in the course of a Voluntary Winding-Up, the Court can review the voluntary Liquidator's remuneration.[1]

(7) *Procedure at Final Meetings*

The Member's meeting is a general meeting of the Company. The Winding-Up rules do not apply and procedure is governed by the Articles (except as to quorum, see below). Procedure at the Creditors' meeting is governed by Rules 127–156.

(8) *Return of Final Meetings*

Within one week of the meetings, the Liquidator must file with the Registrar of Companies his Final Account and a Return of the Meetings (s.290(2), s.300(3)). (Forms on pages 161 and 166). If no quorum was present at either of the meetings, the Liquidator will make a return that the meeting was duly summoned and that there was no quorum, and the requirements as to the making of the return will be deemed to have been complied with (s.290(3), s.300(3)). The Liquidator is liable to a fine of one-fifth of the statutory maximum on summary conviction, i.e. currently a fine of £200, or in the event of further convictions in respect of continued contravention a fine of one-fiftieth of such maximum for each day in which he is in default, i.e. currently a fine of £20 per day: (s.290(4)(5), s.300(4)(5)).[2]

(9) *Dissolution*

The Registrar will register the Account and Return and *three months* after the date of registration the Company is deemed to be dissolved: s.290(4) and s.300(4). The Court can order *deferment* of the date of dissolution on the application of the Liquidator or any person interested: s.290(4) and s.300(4), and within *two years after*

[1] *Re Mortimers (London) Limited* [1937] 2 All E.R. 364.
[2] As amended by the Companies Act 1980.

the dissolution the Court can declare the dissolution void, on the application of the Liquidator or any person interested: s.352. A solicitor, acting for a client, is not a "person interested".[1]

The object of section 352 is to cater for assets or liabilities which have been overlooked, and the power of the Court to declare a dissolution void will not be exercised so as to secure a legacy which had never been an asset of the Company,[2] nor for the benefit of someone who acquired an interest after the date of dissolution.[3] The *two-year* period under s.352 runs from the date of dissolution to the date of commencement of proceedings[4] and should be contrasted with the twenty-year period for application under s.353(6) for restoration to the Register, where a company has been struck off the Register by the Registrar of Companies under s.353.

Under s.353 a Company may be struck off the Register of Companies where the Registrar of Companies has reasonable cause to believe that the Company is not carrying on business or in operation, or, where the Company is being wound-up, no Liquidator is acting or the affairs of the Company are fully wound-up and the returns required to be made by the Liquidator have not been made for a period of six consecutive months.

Where a dissolution is declared void under s.352, the effect is to put the Company in the position which it occupied before the dissolution and property which had vested in the Crown passes back to the Company, as though it had never left it.[5] The Court will declare a dissolution void to enable the prosecution of a personal injuries claim against the Company without prejudice to any defence that the Applicant's claim was statute-barred.[6] However, an action which is pending at the date of dissolution appears not to survive so as to become effective again by virtue of an order under s.352.[7]

An Order under s.352 does not validate acts purportedly done on behalf of the Company while the Company was dissolved.[7] Where the Company is restored on the Register under s.353(6), however, the effect of such restoration is that the Company is deemed to have continued in existence as if its name had not been struck off. Thus

[1] *Re Roehampton Swimming Pool Limited* [1968] 1 W.L.R. 1693.

[2] *Re Servers of the Blind League* [1960] 1 W.L.R. 564.

[3] *Re New Timbiqui Gold Mines Limited* [1961] Ch. 319.

[4] *Re Scad Limited* [1941] Ch. 386.

[5] *Re C. W. Dixon Limited* [1947] Ch. 251.

[6] *Re B.B.H. (Middletons) Limited* (1970) 114 *Sol. J.* 431.

[7] *Foster Yates & Thorn Ltd.* v *H. W. Edgehill Equipment Ltd.* (1978) *The Times* 30th November (C.A.)

[8] *Morris* v *Harris* [1927] A.C. 252.

where a Company is solvent the Court can restore its name to the Register and thereby validate a legal charge purportedly created after the Company had been struck off.[1]

(10) *Bona Vacantia*

On dissolution, all assets, other than those held in trust, become *bona vacantia* and pass to the Crown: s.354. Where the Company was a trustee of property on dissolution a vesting order can be made under s.44 of the Trustee Act 1925 vesting the property either in new trustees or in those beneficially entitled to it.[2]

The Crown is entitled to *disclaim* any such property by notice from the Treasury Solicitor within twelve months of its coming to his notice: s.355.

[1] *Re Boxco Limited* [1970] Ch. 442.
[2] *Re Strathblaine Estates Limited* [1948] Ch. 226.

Appendix 1 RULES

THE COMPANIES (WINDING UP) RULES, 1949,[1] APPLICABLE IN A VOLUNTARY WINDING UP

S.I. 1949 No. 330

Made .. .. .. *23rd February,* 1949.

PRELIMINARY

Interpretation of Terms

1. In these Rules, unless the context or subject-matter otherwise requires:—

"The Act" means the Companies Act, 1948.

"The Company" means a company which is being wound up, or against which proceedings to have it wound up or proceedings under section 210 of the Act have been commenced.

"Judge" means in the High Court the Judge who for the time being exercises the jurisdiction of the High Court to wind up Companies, and in any County Court the Judge thereof.

"Prescribed" in relation to fees or charges means prescribed by the Rules of the Supreme Court.

"Proceedings" means the proceedings in the winding up of a Company under the Act, or proceedings under section 210 of the Act.

"Registrar" means in the High Court any of the Registrars in Bankruptcy of the High Court, and any person who shall be appointed to fill the office of Registrar under these Rules, and where a winding up of a Company is in the District Registry of Leeds, Liverpool, Manchester, Newcastle-upon-Tyne or Preston means the District Registrar; and in a County Court where there are joint Registrars means either of such Registrars, or a Deputy Registrar, and in any Court other than the High Court, means the

[1] These rules are set out as amended by the Companies (Winding-Up) Amendment Rules 1957–1979.

officer of the Court whose duty it is to exercise in relation to a winding up the functions which in the High Court are exercised by a Registrar or Master.

"The Rules" means these Rules, and includes the prescribed Forms.

"Sealed" means sealed with the seal of the Court.

"Taxing Officer" means the officer of the Court whose duty it is to tax costs in the proceedings of the Court under its ordinary jurisdiction.

Unless the context otherwise requires words or expressions contained in these Rules shall bear the same meaning as in the Act or any statutory modification thereof.

Application of Rules

2.—(1) Subject to the limitations hereinafter mentioned, these Rules shall apply to the proceedings in every winding up under the Act which shall commence on and after the date on which these Rules come into operation and to all proceedings under section 210 of the Act, and they shall also, so far as practicable, and subject to any general or special order of the Court, apply to all proceedings which shall be taken or instituted after the said date in the winding up of a company which commenced on or after the first day of January, 1891.

(2) Rules which from their nature and subject matter are, or which by the head lines above the group in which they are contained or by their terms are made applicable only to the proceedings in a winding up by the Court, or only to such proceedings and to proceedings in a creditors' voluntary winding up, shall not apply to the proceedings in a voluntary winding up, or, as the case may be, in a member's voluntary winding up, whether any such voluntary winding up is or is not being continued under the supervision of the Court.

(3) Rules which from their nature and subject matter are, or which by the head lines above the group in which they are contained or by their terms are made applicable only to the proceedings in a winding up, whether by the Court or voluntarily or subject to the supervision of the Court, shall not apply to proceedings under section 210 of the Act.

Use of Forms in Appendix

3. The forms in the Appendix, where applicable, and where they are not applicable, forms of the like character, with such variations as circumstances may require, shall be used. Where such forms are applicable, any costs occasioned by the use of any other or more prolix forms shall be borne by or disallowed to the party using the same, unless the Court shall otherwise direct:

Provided that the Board of Trade may from time to time alter any forms which relate to matters of an administrative and not of a judicial character, or substitute new forms in lieu thereof. Where the Board of Trade alters any form, or substitutes any new form in lieu of a form prescribed by these Rules, such altered or substituted form shall be published in the *London Gazette*.

PROCEEDINGS BY OR AGAINST DIRECTORS, PROMOTERS, AND OFFICERS

Applications by or against delinquent directors, promoters, and officers

68.—(1) An application made to the Court under any of the following provisions of the Act:—

(*a*) Section 333.
(*b*) Subsections (1) or (2) of section 332.
(*c*) Section 188.
(*d*) Subsection (2) of section 448.

or under section 9 of the Insolvency Act 1976 shall in any court other than the High Court be made by motion to the Court. In the High Court the application shall be made by a summons returnable in the first instance in Chambers. The summons shall state the nature of the declaration or order for which application is made, and the grounds of the application, and, unless otherwise ordered, shall be served, in the manner in which an originating summons is required by the Rules of the Supreme Court to be served, on every person against whom an order is sought, not less than fourteen days before the day named in the summons for hearing the application. Where any such application is made by summons no affidavit or report shall be filed before the return of the summons.

(2) On the return of the summons the Court may give such directions as it shall think fit as to whether points of claim and defence are to be delivered, as to the taking of evidence wholly or in part by affidavit or orally, as to the cross examination either before the Judge on the hearing in Court or in Chambers of any deponents to affidavits in support of or in opposition to the application, as to any report it may require the Official Receiver or Liquidator to make and generally as to the procedure on the summons and for the hearing thereof.

(3) Where any such order as is mentioned in paragraph (2) of this Rule has directed that points of claim and defence shall be delivered then if subsequently to such order and before the summons has been set down for trial or adjourned to the Judge either party wishes to apply for any further direction as to any interlocutory matter or thing he shall restore the summons to the Registrar's list and shall give two clear days' notice in writing to the other party stating the grounds of the application. A copy of such notice shall be filed with the Registrar two clear days before the day for which the summons is restored.

Notice of Application

69. Where the application is made by motion the Court may at any time before making an order require the Official Receiver or Liquidator to furnish to the Court a report with respect to any facts or matters which are in his opinion relevant to the application and may give any directions it may see fit with regard to any of the matters mentioned in paragraph (2) of the last preceding Rule. Notice of any such intended motion shall be served on every person against whom an order is sought, not less than eight days before the day named in the notice for hearing the motion. A copy of every report and affidavit intended to be used in support of the motion shall be served on every person to whom notice of motion is given not less than four days before the hearing of the motion.

Hearing of Application

70.—(1) Where any application under section 188 of the Act or under section 9 of the Insolvency Act 1976 is made or heard after a public examination under section 270 of the Act has been held before the Registrar or any of the persons mentioned in subsection (9) of the said section 270, then such application shall be heard and determined by such Registrar or other person unless—

(*a*) the Judge shall otherwise direct, or

(*b*) in the case of an application by the Secretary of State under the said section 9 the public examination was directed to be held by a Court other than the High Court.

The Judge shall personally hear all other applications under the said section 188 or the said section 9:

Provided that in the High Court the Judge may direct that such applications or any of them shall be heard and determined by the Registrar.

(2) Where any order has been made under the said section 188, any application for leave arising out of such order shall be made to the Court having jurisdiction to wind up the company as respects which leave is sought.

(3) An application for leave arising out of an order made under the said section 9 shall be made to the Court by which the order was made.

Disclaimer

Forms 35 *and* 36

75.—(1) (*a*) An application for leave to disclaim any property of a company under section 323 (1) of the Act shall be made by summons to which all persons interested who have not consented to leave to disclaim being granted shall be made respondents.

(*b*) Where all persons interested have consented to leave to disclaim being granted, the application may be made by *ex parte* summons.

(*c*) A summons under this Rule shall be supported by an affidavit stating the names and addresses of all persons interested and the nature of their interests, and verifying any relevant consents.

(*d*) The applicant shall serve the summons and a copy of the affidavit upon every respondent not less than seven clear days before the day named in the summons for the hearing of the application.

(*e*) Where an application under this Rule is made by originating summons, no appearance need be entered to the summons.

(2) Where a Liquidator disclaims a leasehold interest he shall forthwith file the disclaimer at the office of the Registrar. The disclaimer shall contain particulars of the interest disclaimed and a statement of the persons to whom notice of the disclaimer has been given. Until the disclaimer is filed by the Liquidator the disclaimer shall be inoperative. A disclaimer shall be in the Form No. 35 and a notice of disclaimer in the Form No. 36 in the Appendix with such variations as circumstances may require.

(3) Where any person claims to be interested in any part of the property of a Company which the Liquidator wishes to disclaim he shall at the request of the Liquidator furnish a statement of the interest so claimed by him.

Vesting of Disclaimed Property

76.—(1) Any application under subsection (6) of section 323 of the Act for an order for the vesting of any disclaimed property in or the delivery of any such property to any persons shall be supported by the affidavit filed on the application for leave to disclaim such property.

(2) Where such an application as aforesaid relates to disclaimed property of a leasehold nature and it appears that there is any mortgagee by demise (including a chargee by way of legal mortgage), or under-lessee of such property, the Court may direct that notice shall be given to such mortgagee or under-lessee that, if he does not elect to accept and apply for such a vesting order as aforesaid upon the terms required by the above-mentioned subsection and imposed by the Court within a time to be fixed by the Court and stated in the notice, he will be excluded from all interest in and security upon the property, and the Court may adjourn the application for such notice to be given and for such mortgagee or under-lessee to be added as a party to and served with the application and if he sees fit to make such election and application as is mentioned in the notice. If at the expiration of the time so fixed by the Court such mortgagee or underlessee fails to make such election and application, the Court may make an order vesting the property in the applicant and excluding such mortgagee or under-lessee from all interest in or security upon the property.

Proofs

Mode of Proof

92.—(1) A debt may be proved in a winding-up by the Court by delivering or sending through the post in a pre-paid letter to the Official Receiver or, if a Liquidator has been appointed, to the Liquidator—

(*a*) in any case in which the Official Receiver or Liquidator so requires, an affidavit verifying the debt; and

(*b*) in any other case, an unsworn claim to the debt.

(2) In any other winding-up the Liquidator may require a debt to be proved by delivering or sending to him through the post in a pre-paid letter either an unsworn claim to the debt or an affidavit verifying the debt, as he may direct.

Verification of Proof

93. A proof of debt may be made by the creditor himself or by some person authorised by or on behalf of the creditor. If made by a person so authorised, it shall state his authority and means of knowledge.

Contents of Proof. Form 59

94. A proof of debt shall contain or refer to a statement of account showing the particulars of the debt, and shall specify the vouchers, if any, by which the same can be substantiated. The Official Receiver or Liquidator to whom the proof is sent may at any time call for the production of the vouchers.

Statement of Security

95. A proof of debt shall state whether the creditor is or is not a secured creditor.

Costs of Proof

97. A creditor shall bear the cost of proving his debt unless the Court otherwise orders.

Discount

98. A creditor proving his debt shall deduct therefrom (*a*) any discount which he may have agreed to allow for payment in cash in excess of five per centum on the net amount of his claim and (*b*) all trade discounts.

Periodical Payments

99. When any rent or other payment falls due at stated periods, and the order or resolution to wind up is made at any time other than one of those periods, the persons entitled to the rent or payment may prove for a proportionate part thereof up to the date of the winding-up order or resolution as if the rent or payment grew due from day to day. Provided that where the Liquidator remains in occupation of premises demised to a Company which is being wound up, nothing herein contained shall prejudice or affect the right of the landlord of such premises to claim payment by the Company, or the Liquidator, of rent during the period of the Company's or the Liquidator's occupation.

Interest

100. On any debt or sum certain, payable at a certain time or otherwise, whereon interest is not reserved or agreed for, and which is overdue at the date of the commencement of the winding up, the creditor may prove for interest at a rate not exceeding four per centum per annum to that date from the time when the debt or sum was payable, if the debt or sum is payable by virtue of a written instrument at a certain time, and if payable otherwise, then from the time when a demand in writing has been made, giving notice that interest will be claimed from the date of the demand until the time of payment.

Proof for Debt Payable at a Future Time

101. A creditor may prove for a debt not payable at the date of the winding-up order or resolution, as if it were payable presently, and may receive dividends equally with the other creditors, deducting only thereout a rebate of interest at the rate of five per centum per annum computed from the declaration of a dividend to the time when the debt would have become payable according to the terms on which it was contracted.

Proof under Section 319

102. Unless the Official Receiver or Liquidator shall in any special case otherwise direct formal proof of the debts mentioned in paragraph (*e*) of subsection (1) of section 319 of the Act shall not be required.

Workmen's Wages. Form 60

103. In any case in which it appears that there are numerous claims for wages or accrued holiday remuneration by workmen and others employed by the Company, it shall be sufficient if one proof for all such claims is made either by a foreman or by some other person on behalf of all such creditors. Such proof shall have annexed thereto as forming part thereof, a schedule setting forth the names of the workmen and others, and the amounts severally due to them. Any proof made in compliance with this Rule shall have the same effect as if separate proofs had been made by each of the said workmen and others.

Production of Bills of Exchange and Promissory Notes

104. Where a creditor seeks to prove in respect of a bill of exchange, promissory note, or other negotiable instrument or security on which the Company is liable, such bill of exchange, note, instrument, or security must, subject to any special order of the Court made to the contrary, be produced to the Official Receiver, Chairman of a meeting or Liquidator, as the case may be, and be marked by him before the proof can be admitted either for voting or for any purpose.

ADMISSION AND REJECTION OF PROOFS AND PREFERENTIAL CLAIMS AND APPEAL TO THE COURT.

Notice to Creditors to Prove

106—(1) Subject to the provisions of the Act, and unless otherwise ordered by the Court, the Liquidator in any winding up may from time to time fix a certain day, which shall be not less than fourteen days from the date of the notice, on or before which the creditors of the Company are to prove their debts or claims, and to establish any title they may have to priority under section 319 of the Act, or to be excluded from the benefit of any distribution made before such debts are proved, or as the case may be from objecting to such distribution.

(2) The Liquidator shall give notice in writing of the day so fixed by advertisement in such newspaper as he shall consider convenient, and in a winding up by the Court to every person mentioned, in the Statement of Affairs as a creditor, who has not proved his debt, and to every person mentioned in the Statement of Affairs as a preferential creditor whose claim to be a preferential creditor has not been established and is not admitted, and in any other winding up to the last known address or place of abode of each person who, to the knowledge of the Liquidator, claims to be a creditor or preferential creditor of the Company and whose claim has not been admitted.

(3) All the Rules hereinafter set out as to admission and rejection of proofs shall apply with the necessary variations to any such claim to priority as aforesaid.

Examination of Proof. Form 61

107. The Liquidator shall examine every proof of debt lodged with him, and the grounds of the debt, and in writing admit or reject it, in whole or in part, or require further evidence in support of it. If he rejects a proof he shall state in writing to the creditor the grounds of the rejection.

Appeal by Creditor

108. If a creditor or contributory is dissatisfied with the decision of the Liquidator in respect of a proof, the Court may, on the application of the creditor or contributory, reverse or vary the decision; but, subject to the power of the Court to extend the time, no application to reverse or vary the decision of the Liquidator in a winding up by the Court rejecting a proof sent to him by a creditor, or person claiming to be a creditor, shall be entertained, unless notice of the application is given before the expiration of twenty-one days from the date of the service of the notice of rejection.

Expunging at Instance of Liquidator

109. If the Liquidator thinks that a proof has been improperly admitted, the Court may, on the application of the Liquidator, after notice to the creditor who made the proof, expunge the proof or reduce its amount.

Expunging at Instance of Creditor

110. The Court may also expunge or vary a proof upon the application of a creditor or contributory if the Liquidator declines to interfere in the matter.

GENERAL MEETINGS OF CREDITORS AND CONTRIBUTORIES IN RELATION TO WINDING UP BY THE COURT AND OF CREDITORS IN RELATION TO A CREDITOR'S VOLUNTARY WINDING UP

Liquidator's Meetings of Creditors and Contributories

127.—(1) In addition to the first meetings of creditors and contributories and in addition also to meetings of creditors and contributories directed to be held by the Court under section 346 of the Act (hereinafter referred to as Court meetings of creditors and contributories), the Liquidator in any winding up by the Court may himself from time to time subject to the provisions of the Act and the control of the Court summon, hold and conduct meetings of the creditors or contributories (hereinafter referred to as Liquidator's meetings of creditors and contributories) for the purpose of ascertaining their wishes in all matters relating to the winding up.

(2) In any creditors' voluntary winding up the Liquidator may himself from time to time summon, hold and conduct meetings of creditors for the purpose of ascertaining their wishes in all matters relating to the winding up (such meetings and all meetings of

creditors which a Liquidator or a Company is by the Act required to convene in or immediately before such a voluntary winding up and all meetings convened by a creditor in a voluntary winding up under these Rules are hereinafter called voluntary liquidation meetings).

Application of Rules as to Meetings

128. Except where and so far as the nature of the subject-matter or the context may otherwise require the Rules as to meetings hereinafter set out shall apply to first meetings, Court meetings, Liquidator's meetings of creditors and contributories, and voluntary liquidation meetings, but so nevertheless that the said Rules shall take effect as to first meetings subject and without prejudice to any express provisions of the Act and as to Court meetings subject and without prejudice to any express directions of the Court.

Summoning of Meetings. Form 75

129.—(1) The Official Receiver or Liquidator shall summon all meetings of creditors and contributories by giving not less than seven days' notice of the time and place thereof in the Gazette and in a local paper; and shall not less than seven days before the day appointed for the meeting send by post to every person appearing by the Company's books to be a creditor of the Company notice of the meeting of creditors, and to every person appearing by the Company's books or otherwise to be a contributory of the Company notice of the meeting of contributories.

(2) The notice to each creditor shall be sent to the address given in his proof, or if he has not proved to the address given in the Statement of Affairs of the Company, if any, or to such other address as may be known to the person summoning the meeting. The notice to each contributory shall be sent to the address mentioned in the Company's books as the address of such contributory, or to such other address as may be known to the person summoning the meeting.

(3) In the case of meetings under section 297 of the Act the continuing Liquidator or if there is no continuing Liquidator any creditor may summon the meeting.

(4) This Rule shall not apply to meetings under section 293 or section 300 of the Act.

Proof of Notice. Forms 76 *and* 77

130. A certificate by the Official Receiver or other officer of the

Court, or by the clerk of any such person, or an affidavit by the Liquidator, or creditor, or his solicitor, or the clerk of either of such persons, or as the case may be by some officer of the Company or its solicitor or the clerk of such Company or solicitor, that the notice of any meeting has been duly posted, shall be sufficient evidence of such notice having been duly sent to the person to whom the same was addressed.

Place of Meetings

131. Every meeting shall be held at such place as is in the opinion of the person convening the same most convenient for the majority of the creditors or contributories or both. Different times or places or both may if thought expedient be named for the meetings of creditors and for the meetings of contributories.

Costs of Calling Meetings

132.—(1) The costs of summoning a meeting of creditors or contributories at the instance of any person other than the Official Receiver or Liquidator shall be paid by the person at whose instance it is summoned who shall before the meeting is summoned deposit with the Official Receiver or Liquidator (as the case may be) such sum as may be required by the Official Receiver or Liquidator as security for the payment of such costs.

(2) The costs of summoning a meeting under paragraph (1) above, including all disbursements for printing, stationery, postage and the hire of room, shall be calculated in accordance with paragraph (3) hereof and shall be repaid out of the assets of the Company if the Court shall by order or if the creditors or contributories (as the case may be) shall by resolution so direct.

(3) Where the number of creditors or contributories to whom notice is required to be sent does not exceed 25, the costs shall be £25, and for every addition of 10 such creditors or contributories or part thereof there shall be added £7·50; but the costs in respect of an adjourned meeting shall be calculated at half of this rate.

(4) This rule shall not apply to meetings under section 293 or 297 of the Act.

Chairman of Meeting. *Form* 78

133. Where a meeting is summoned by the Official Receiver or the Liquidator, he or someone nominated by him shall be Chairman of the meeting. At every other meeting of creditors or contributories the Chairman shall be such person as the meeting by resolution shall appoint. This Rule shall not apply to meetings under section 293 of the Act.

Ordinary Resolution of Creditors and Contributories

134. At a meeting of creditors a resolution shall be deemed to be passed when a majority in number and value of the creditors present personally or by proxy and voting on the resolution have voted in favour of the resolution, and at a meeting of the contributories a resolution shall be deemed to be passed when a majority in number and value of the contributories present personally or by proxy, and voting on the resolution, have voted in favour of the resolution, the value of the contributories being determined according to the number of votes conferred on each contributory by the regulations of the Company.

Non-reception of Notice by a Creditor

136. Where a meeting of creditors or contributories is summoned by notice the proceedings and resolutions at the meeting shall unless the Court otherwise orders be valid notwithstanding that some creditors or contributories may not have received the notice sent to them.

Adjournments. Form 79

137. The Chairman may with the consent of the meeting adjourn it from time to time and from place to place, but the adjourned meeting shall be held at the same place as the original meeting unless in the resolution for adjournment another place is specified or unless the Court otherwise orders.

Quorum

138.—(1) A meeting may not act for any purpose except the election of a chairman, the proving of debts and the adjournment of the meeting unless there are present or represented thereat in the case of a creditors' meeting at least three creditors entitled to vote or in the case of a meeting of contributories at least three contributories or all the creditors entitled to vote or all the contributories if the number of creditors entitled to vote or the number of contributories as the case may be shall not exceed three.

(2) If within half an hour from the time appointed for the meeting a quorum of creditors or contributories, as the case may be, is not

present or represented, the meeting shall be adjourned to the same day in the following week at the same time and place or to such other day or time or place as the chairman may appoint, but so that the day appointed shall be not less than seven nor more than twenty-one days from the day from which the meeting was adjourned.

Cases in which Creditors may not Vote

140. A creditor shall not vote in respect of any unliquidated or contingent debt or any debt the value of which is not ascertained, nor shall a creditor vote in respect of any debt on or secured by a current bill of exchange or promissory note held by him unless he is willing to treat the liability to him thereon of every person who is liable thereon antecedently to the Company, and against whom a Receiving Order in Bankruptcy has not been made, as a security in his hands, and to estimate the value thereof, and for the purposes of voting, but not for the purposes of dividend, to deduct it from his proof.

Votes of Secured Creditors

141. For the purpose of voting, a secured creditor shall, unless he surrenders his security, state in his proof or in a voluntary liquidation in such a statement as is hereinafter mentioned the particulars of his security, the date when it was given, and the value at which he assesses it, and shall be entitled to vote only in respect of the balance (if any) due to him after deducting the value of his security. If he votes in respect of his whole debt he shall be deemed to have surrendered his security, unless the Court on application is satisfied that the omission to value the security has arisen from inadvertence.

Creditor Required to give up Security

142. The Official Receiver or Liquidator may, within twenty-eight days after a proof or in a voluntary liquidation a statement estimating the value of a security as aforesaid has been used in voting at a meeting, require the creditor to give up the security for the benefit of the creditors generally on payment of the value so estimated with an addition thereto of twenty per cent.: Provided that where a creditor has valued his security he may at any time before being required to give it up correct the valuation by a new proof and deduct the new value from his debt, but in that case the said addition of twenty per cent. shall not be made if the security is required to be given up.

Admission and Rejection of Proofs for Purpose of Voting

143. The Chairman shall have power to admit or reject a proof for the purpose of voting, but his decision shall be subject to appeal to the Court. If he is in doubt whether a proof shall be admitted or rejected he shall mark it as objected to and allow the creditor to vote subject to the vote being declared invalid in the event of the objection being sustained.

Statement of Security

144. For the purpose of voting at any voluntary liquidation meetings, a secured creditor shall, unless he surrender his security, lodge with the Liquidator or, where there is no Liquidator, at the Registered Office of the Company, before the meeting a statement giving the particulars of his security, the date when it was given and the value at which he assesses it.

Minutes of Meeting

145.—(1) The Chairman shall cause minutes of the proceedings at the meeting to be drawn up and fairly entered in a book kept for that purpose and the minutes shall be signed by him or by the Chairman of the next ensuing meeting.

Form 74

(2) A list of creditors and contributories present at every meeting shall be made and kept as in Form 74 in the Appendix.

Proxies in Relation to a Winding Up by the Court and to Meetings of Creditors in a Creditors' Voluntary Winding Up

Proxies

146. A creditor or a contributory may vote either in person or by proxy. Where a person is authorised in manner provided by section 139 of the Act to represent a corporation at any meeting of creditors or contributories such person shall produce to the Official Receiver or Liquidator or other the Chairman of the meeting a copy of the resolution so authorising him. Such copy must either be under the seal of the corporation or must be certified to be a true copy by the secretary or a director of the corporation. The succeeding Rules as to proxies shall not (unless otherwise directed by the Court) apply to a Court meeting of creditors or contributories prior to the first meeting.

Form of Proxies. Forms 80 *and* 81

147. Every instrument of proxy shall be in accordance with the appropriate form in the Appendix.

Forms of Proxy to be sent with Notices

148. General and special forms of proxy shall be sent to the creditors and contributories with the notice summoning the meeting, and neither the name nor description of the Official Receiver or Liquidator or any other person shall be printed or inserted in the body of any instrument of proxy before it is so sent.

General Proxies

149. A creditor or a contributory may give a general proxy to any person.

Special Proxies

150. A creditor or a contributory may give a special proxy to any person to vote at any specified meeting or adjournment thereof—

(*a*) for or against the appointment or continuance in office of any specified person as Liquidator or Member of the Committee of Inspection; and

(*b*) on all questions relating to any matter other than those above referred to and arising at the meeting or an adjournment thereof.

Solicitation by Liquidator to Obtain Proxies

151. Where it appears to the satisfaction of the Court that any solicitation has been used by or on behalf of a Liquidator in obtaining proxies or in procuring his appointment as Liquidator except by the direction of a meeting of creditors or contributories, the Court if it thinks fit may order that no remuneration be allowed to the person by whom or on whose behalf the solicitation was exercised notwithstanding any resolution of the Committee of Inspection or of the creditors or contributories to the contrary.

Proxies to Official Receiver or Liquidator

152. A creditor or a contributory in a winding up by the Court may appoint the Official Receiver or Liquidator and in a voluntary winding up the Liquidator or if there is no Liquidator the Chairman of a meeting to act as his general or special proxy.

Holder of Proxy not to Vote on Matter in which he is Financially Interested

153. No person acting either under a general or a special proxy shall vote in favour of any resolution which would directly or indirectly place himself, his partner or employer in a position to receive any remuneration out of the estate of the Company otherwise than as a creditor rateably with the other creditors of the Company; provided that where any person holds special proxies to vote for an application to the Court in favour of the appointment of himself as Liquidator he may use the said proxies and vote accordingly.

Proxies. Forms 80 *and* 81

154.—(1) A proxy intended to be used at the first meeting of creditors or contributories, or an adjournment thereof, shall be lodged with the Official Receiver not later than the time mentioned for that purpose in the notice convening the meeting or the adjourned meeting, which time shall be not earlier than twelve o'clock at noon of the day but one before, nor later than twelve o'clock at noon of the day before the day appointed for such meeting, unless the Court otherwise directs.

(2) In every other case a proxy shall be lodged with the Official Receiver or Liquidator in a winding up by the Court, with the Company at its Registered Office for a meeting under section 293 of the Act, and with the Liquidator or if there is no Liquidator with the person named in the notice convening the meeting to receive the same in a voluntary winding up not later than four o'clock in the afternoon of the day before the meeting or adjourned meeting at which it is to be used.

(3) No person shall be appointed a general or special proxy who is a minor.

Filling in where Creditor Blind or Incapable

156. The proxy of a creditor blind or incapable of writing may be accepted if such creditor has attached his signature or mark thereto in the presence of a witness, who shall add to his signature his description and residence: Provided that such witness shall have certified at the foot of the proxy that all such insertions have been made at the request and in the presence of the creditor before he attached his signature or mark.

Limit of Remuneration

160. Except as provided by the Act or the Rules, a Liquidator shall not under any circumstances whatever make any arrangement for, or accept from any solicitor, auctioneer, or any other person connected with the Company of which he is Liquidator, or who is employed in or in connection with the winding up of the Company, any gift, remuneration, or pecuniary or other consideration of benefit whatever beyond the remuneration to which under the Act and the Rules he is entitled as Liquidator, nor shall he make any arrangement for giving up, or give up any part of such remuneration to any such solicitor, auctioneer, or other person.

Dealings with Assets

161. Neither the Liquidator, nor any member of the Committee of Inspection of a Company shall, while acting as Liquidator or member of such committee, except by leave of the Court, either directly or indirectly, by himself or any employer, partner, clerk, agent, or servant, become purchaser of any part of the Company's assets. Any such purchase made contrary to the provisions of this Rule may be set aside by the Court on the application of the Board of Trade in a winding up by the Court or of any creditor or contributory in any winding up, and the Court may make such order as to costs as the Court shall think fit.

Restriction on Purchase of Goods by Liquidator

162. Where the Liquidator carries on the business of the Company, he shall not, without the express sanction of the Court, purchase goods for the carrying on of such business from any person whose connection with him is of such a nature as would result in his obtaining any portion of the profit (if any) arising out of the transaction.

Committee of Inspection not to make Profit

163. No member of a Committee of Inspection shall, except under and with the sanction of the Court, directly or indirectly, by himself, or any employer, partner, clerk, agent, or servant, be entitled to derive any profit from any transaction arising out of the winding up or to receive out of the assets any payment for services rendered by him in connection with the administration of the assets, or for any goods supplied by him to the Liquidator for or on account of the Company. In a winding up by the Court if it appears to the Board of Trade or in a voluntary winding up if it appears to the Committee of

Inspection or to any meeting of creditors or contributories that any profit or payment has been made contrary to the provisions of this Rule, they may disallow such payment or recover such profit, as the case may be, on the audit of the Liquidator's accounts or otherwise.

Costs of Obtaining Sanction of Court

164. In any case in which the sanction of the Court is obtained under the two last preceding Rules, the cost of obtaining such sanction shall be borne by the person in whose interest such sanction is obtained, and shall not be payable out of the Company's assets.

Sanction of Payments to Committee

165. Where the sanction of the Court to a payment to a member of a Committee of Inspection for services rendered by him in connection with the administration of the Company's assets is obtained, the order of the Court shall specify the nature of the services, and such sanction shall only be given where the service performed is of a special nature. Except by the express sanction of the Court no remuneration shall, under any circumstances, be paid to a member of a Committee for services rendered by him in the discharge of the duties attaching to his office as a member of such Committee.

Office of Liquidator Vacated by his Insolvency

168. If a Receiving Order in Bankruptcy is made against a Liquidator, he shall thereby vacate his office, and for the purposes of the application of the Act and Rules shall be deemed to have been removed.

Payments Into and Out of a Bank

Payments out of Bank of England

169. All payments out of the Insolvency Services Account shall be made in such manner as the Board of Trade may from time to time direct.

Books to be Kept in a Creditors' Voluntary Winding Up

172.—(3) In a creditors' voluntary winding up the Liquidator shall keep such books as the Committee of Inspection or if there is no such Committee as the creditors direct and all books kept by the Liquidator shall be submitted to the Committee of Inspection or if there is no such Committee to the creditors with any other books documents papers and accounts in his possession relating to his office as Liquidator or to the company as and when the Committee of Inspection or if there is no such Committee the creditors direct.

Investment of Funds

Investment of Assets in Securities and Realisation of Securities
Forms 84 *and* 85

173.—(1) Where in a winding up by the Court or in a creditors' voluntary winding up the Committee of Inspection are of opinion that any part of the cash balance standing to the credit of the account of the Company should be invested, they shall sign a certificate and request, and the Liquidator shall transmit such certificate and request to the Board of Trade.

(2) Where the Committee of Inspection in any such winding up are of opinion that it is advisable to sell any of the securities in which the moneys of the Company's assets are invested they shall sign a certificate and request to that effect, and the Liquidator shall transmit such certificate and request to the Board of Trade.

(3) Where there is no Committee of Inspection in any such winding up as is mentioned in paragraphs (1) and (2) of this Rule and in every member's voluntary winding up whether under the supervision of the Court or not, if a case has in the opinion of the Liquidator arisen under section 362 of the Act for an investment of funds of the Company or a sale of securities in which the Company's funds have been invested, the Liquidator shall sign and transmit to the Board of Trade a certificate of the facts on which his opinion is founded, and a request to the Board of Trade to make the investment or sale mentioned in the certificate, and the Board of Trade may thereupon, if they think fit, invest or sell the whole or any part of the said funds and securities, as provided in the said section, and the said certificate and request shall be a sufficient authority to the Board of Trade for the said investment or sale.

Final Account in Voluntary Winding Up

Form 110

182. The account required by sections 290 and 300 of the Act to be made up by the Liquidator as soon as the affairs of the Company are fully wound up shall be in form No. 110 in the Appendix.

Costs and Expenses Payable out of the Assets of the Company

195.—(1) The assets of a Company in a winding up by the Court remaining after payment of the fees and expenses properly incurred in preserving, realising or getting in the assets, including where the Company has previously commenced to be wound up voluntarily, such remuneration, costs and expenses as the Court may allow to a Liquidator appointed in such voluntary winding up shall, subject to any order of the Court, and, as regards a winding up to which the provisions of the Stannaries Act, 1887, apply, subject to that Act as modified by the Act, be liable to the following payments, which shall be made in the following order of priority, namely:—

First. The taxed costs of the petition, including the taxed costs of any person appearing on the petition whose costs are allowed by the Court.

Next. The remuneration of the special manager (if any).

Next. The costs and expenses of any person who makes or concurs in making the Company's statement of affairs.

Next. The taxed charges of any shorthand writer appointed to take an examination: Provided that where the shorthand writer is appointed at the instance of the Official Receiver the cost of the shorthand notes shall be deemed to be an expense incurred by the Official Receiver in getting in and realising the assets of the Company.

Next. The necessary disbursements of any Liquidator appointed in the winding up by the Court, other than expenses properly incurred in preserving, realising or getting in the assets heretofore provided for.

Next. The costs of any person properly employed by any such Liquidator.

Next. The remuneration of any such Liquidator.

Next. The actual out-of-pocket expenses necessarily incurred by the Committee of Inspection, subject to the approval of the Board of Trade.

(2) No payments in respect of bills of costs, charges or expenses of solicitors, managers, accountants, auctioneers, brokers or other persons, other than payments for costs, charges or expenses fixed or allowed by the Court under the Act or the Rules, or sanctioned by the Official Receiver under Rule 56, shall be allowed out of the assets of the company unless they have been duly taxed and allowed by the Taxing Officer. The Taxing Officer shall, before passing the bill of costs, charges or expenses of a solicitor satisfy himself that the

appointment of a solicitor to assist the Liquidator in the performance of his duties has been duly sanctioned: Provided that the costs, charges and expenses of any person employed by an Official Receiver or liquidator may, if they are within the scale usually allowed by the Court and do not exceed the sum of £100, be paid and allowed by the Official Receiver or liquidator, as the case may be, without taxation; so, however, that the Secretary of State may require such costs, charges and expenses to be taxed by the Taxing Officer.

(3) Nothing contained in this Rule shall apply to or affect costs which, in the course of legal proceedings by or against a Company which is being wound up by the Court, are ordered by the Court in which such proceedings are pending or a judge thereof to be paid by the Company or the Liquidator, or the rights of the person to whom such costs are payable.

Statements by Liquidator to the Registrar of Companies

Conclusion of Winding Up

196. The winding up of a Company shall, for the purpose of section 342 of the Act, be deemed to be concluded:—

(*a*) in the case of a Company wound up by order of the Court, at the date on which the order dissolving the Company has been reported by the Liquidator to the Registrar of Companies, or at the date of the order of the Board of Trade releasing the Liquidator pursuant to section 251 of the Act.

(*b*) in the case of a Company wound up voluntarily, or under the supervision of the Court, at the date of the dissolution of the Company, unless at such date any funds or assets of the Company remain unclaimed or undistributed in the hands or under the control of the Liquidator, or any person who has acted as Liquidator, in which case the winding up shall not be deemed to be concluded until such funds or assets have either been distributed or paid into the Companies Liquidation Account[1] at the Bank of England.

Times for Sending Liquidator's Statements, and Regulations Applicable Thereto

197. In a voluntary winding up or a winding up under the supervision of the Court, the statements with respect to the

[1] Now the Insolvency Services Account.

proceedings in and position of the liquidation of a Company the winding up of which is not concluded within a year after its commencement shall be sent to the Registrar of Companies twice in every year as follows:—

(1) The first statement, commencing at the date when a Liquidator was first appointed and brought down to the end of twelve months from the commencement of the winding up, shall be sent within 30 days from the expiration of such twelve months, or within such extended period as the Board of Trade may sanction, and the subsequent statements shall be sent at intervals of half a year, each statement being brought down to the end of the half year for which it is sent. In cases in which the assets of the Company have been fully realised and distributed before the expiration of a half-yearly interval a final statement shall be sent forthwith.

Forms 92, 94, 95 *and* 96

(2) Subject to the next succeeding Rule, Form No. 92, and where applicable Forms 94, 95 and 96, with such variations as circumstances may require, shall be used, and the directions specified in the Form (unless the Board of Trade otherwise direct) be observed in reference to every statement.

Form 93

(3) Every statement shall be sent in duplicate, and shall be verified by an affidavit in the Form No. 93, with such variations as circumstances may require.

Affidavit of no Receipts or Payments. *Forms* 92 *and* 93

198. Where, in a voluntary winding up or a winding up under the supervision of the Court, a Liquidator has not during any period for which a statement has to be sent received or paid any money on account of the Company, he shall, at the period when he is required to transmit his statement, send to the Registrar of Companies the prescribed statement in the Form No. 92, in duplicate, containing the particulars therein required with respect to the proceedings in and position of the Liquidation, and with such statement shall also send an affidavit of no receipts or payments in the Form No. 93.

UNCLAIMED FUNDS AND UNDISTRIBUTED ASSETS IN THE HANDS OF A LIQUIDATOR

Payment of Undistributed and Unclaimed Money into Companies Liquidation Account[1]

199.—(1) All money in the hands or under the control of a Liquidator of a Company representing unclaimed dividends, which for six months from the date when the dividend became payable have remained in the hands or under the control of the Liquidator, shall forthwith on the expiration of the six months be paid into the Insolvency Services Account.

(2) In a voluntary winding up or a winding up under the supervision of the Court, all other money in the hands or under the control of a Liquidator of a Company, representing unclaimed or undistributed assets or held by the Company in trust which, under subsection (1) of section 343 of the Act, the Liquidator is to pay into the Insolvency Services Account, shall be ascertained as on the date to which the statement of receipts and payments sent in to the Registrar of Companies is brought down and the amount to be paid to the Insolvency Services Account shall be the minimum balance of such money which the Liquidator has had in his hands or under his control during the six months immediately preceding the date to which the statement is brought down, less such part (if any) thereof as the Board of Trade may authorise him to retain for the immediate purposes of the liquidation. Such amount shall be paid into the Insolvency Services Account within fourteen days from the date to which the statement of account is brought down.

(3) Notwithstanding anything in this Rule, any moneys in the hands of the Liquidator at the date of the dissolution of the Company representing unclaimed or undistributed assets or dividends or held by the Company in trust in respect of dividends or other sums due to any person as a member of the Company shall forthwith be paid by him into the Insolvency Services Account.

(4) A Liquidator, whose duty it is to pay into the Insolvency Services Account at the Bank of England money representing unclaimed or undistributed assets of the Company or held by the Company in trust in respect of dividends or other sums due to any person as a member of the Company, shall apply in such manner as the Board of Trade shall direct to the Board of Trade for a paying-in order, which paying-in order shall be an authority to the Bank of England to receive the payment.

[1] Now the Insolvency Services Account.

(5) In a voluntary winding up or a winding up under the supervision of the Court, money invested or deposited at interest by a Liquidator shall be deemed to be money under his control, and when such money forms part of the minimum balance payable into the Insolvency Services Account pursuant to paragraph (2) of this Rule, the Liquidator shall realise the investment or withdraw the deposit, and shall pay the proceeds into the Insolvency Services Account: Provided that where the money is invested in Government securities, such securities may, with the permission of the Board of Trade, be transferred to the control of the Board of Trade instead of being forthwith realised and the proceeds thereof paid into the Insolvency Services Account. If and when the money represented by the securities is required wholly or in part for the purposes of the liquidation, the Board of Trade may realise the securities wholly or in part and pay the proceeds of realisation into the Insolvency Services Account and deal with the same in the same way as other moneys paid into the said Account may be dealt with.

Liquidator to Furnish Information to Board of Trade. *Form* 97

200. In a voluntary winding up or a winding up under the supervision of the Court, every person who has acted as Liquidator of any Company, whether the liquidation has been concluded or not, shall furnish to the Board of Trade particulars of any money in his hands or under his control representing unclaimed or undistributed assets of the Company or held by the Company in trust in respect of dividends or other sums due to any person as a member of the Company, and such other particulars as the Board of Trade may require for the purpose of ascertaining or getting in any money payable into the Insolvency Services Account at the Bank of England. The Board of Trade may require such particulars to be verified by affidavit.

Board of Trade may Call for Verified Accounts. *Forms* 92, 93 *to* 96

201.—(1) In a voluntary winding up or a winding up under the supervision of the Court, the Board of Trade may at any time order any such person as is mentioned in the preceding Rule to submit to them an account verified by affidavit of the sums received and paid by him as Liquidator of the Company, and may direct and enforce an audit of the account.

(2) For the purposes of section 343 of the Act, and the Rules, the Court has and may exercise all the powers conferred by the Bankruptcy Act, 1914, with respect to the discovery and realisation

of the property of a debtor, and the provisions of Part I of that Act with respect thereto shall, with any necessary modification, apply to proceedings under section 343 of the Act.

Application to the Court for Enforcing an Account, and Getting in Money

202. In a voluntary winding up an application by the Secretary of State for the purpose of ascertaining and getting in money payable into the Bank of England pursuant to section 343 of the Act shall be made to the High Court.

Application for Payment out by Person Entitled

203. An application by a person claiming to be entitled to any money paid into the Bank of England in pursuance of section 343 of the Act, shall be made in such form and manner as the Board of Trade may from time to time direct, and shall, unless the Board of Trade otherwise directs, be accompanied by the certificate of the Liquidator that the person claiming is entitled and such further evidence as the Board of Trade may direct.

Application by Liquidator for Payment out

204. A Liquidator who requires to make payments out of money paid into the Bank of England in pursuance of section 343 of the Act, either by way of distribution or in respect of the cost and expenses of the proceedings, shall apply in such form and manner as the Board of Trade may direct, and the Board of Trade may thereupon either make an order for payment to the Liquidator of the sum required by him for the purposes aforesaid, or may direct cheques to be issued to the Liquidator for transmission to the persons to whom the payments are to be made.

Disposal of Books and Papers

206.—(1) The Board of Trade may order that the books and papers of a Company which has been wound up shall not be destroyed for such period (not exceeding five years from the dissolution of the Company) as the Board thinks proper.

(2) Any creditor or contributory may make representations to the Board with regard to the destruction of such books and papers and may appeal to the Court from any order made by the Board under this Rule.

(3) Subject to any order of the Court, the Board of Trade may by a further order vary or rescind any order made by it under this Rule.

(4) A resolution for the destruction of the books and papers of such a Company within the said period of five years, or any shorter period fixed by an order of the Board in force at the date of such resolution, shall not take effect until the expiration of such period of five years or of such shorter period unless the Board shall otherwise direct.

(5) At least one week's notice shall be given to the Board of Trade of any application to the Court for an order for the destruction of the books and papers of a Company before the expiration of such period of five years or shorter period.

Appeals from Board of Trade and Official Receiver

215. An appeal in the High Court against a decision of the Board of Trade, or an appeal to the Court from an act or decision of the Official Receiver acting otherwise than as Liquidator of a Company, shall be brought within twenty-one days from the time when the decision or act appealed against is done, pronounced or made.

Board of Trade Orders

224. The Board of Trade may from time to time issue general orders or regulations for the purpose of regulating any matters under the Act or the Rules which are of an administrative and not a judicial character. Judicial notice shall be taken of any general orders or regulations which are printed by the King's Printer and purport to be issued under the authority of the Board of Trade.

Enlargement or abridgment of time

225. The Court may, in any case in which it shall see fit, extend or abridge the time appointed by the Rules or fixed by any order of the Court for doing any act or taking any proceeding.

Formal Defect not to Invalidate Proceedings

226.—(1) No proceedings under the Act or the Rules shall be invalidated by any formal defect or by any irregularity, unless the Court before which an objection is made to the proceeding is of opinion that substantial injustice has been caused by the defect or irregularity and that the injustice cannot be remedied by any order of that Court.

(2) No defect or irregularity in the appointment or election of an Official Receiver, Liquidator or member of a Committee of Inspection shall vitiate any act done by him in good faith.

Annulment

229. The Companies (Winding Up) Rules, 1929, and all rules amending or supplementing the same and the forms thereby prescribed, are hereby revoked and annulled, except so far as they relate to any winding up which commenced before the first day of January, 1891: Provided that such revocation and annulment shall not prejudice or affect anything done or suffered before the date on which these Rules come into operation under any rule or order which is hereby revoked and annulled and that no rule or practice which was annulled or repealed by the said rules and orders shall be revived by reason of the revocation and annulment hereby effected.

Short Title and Commencement

230. These Rules may be cited as the Companies (Winding Up) Rules, 1949. They shall come into operation on the fourteenth day of March, 1949.

NOTE. Wherever "Registered Post" is referred to in these Rules the Recorded Delivery Service may be used as an alternative: *The Companies (Winding Up) (Amendment) Rules 1962* (S.I. 1962 No. 296).

Appendix 2 FORMS

Forms and Specimens for a Voluntary Winding-Up are printed in the order in which they will normally be used.

The source of each form and its number is indicated as follows:

Appendix to the Rules	(R)
Companies (Forms) Regulations 1979	(F)
Published by Jordan & Sons Limited	(J)

Specimens are described as such and the words "Members" or "Creditors" are added to all forms to indicate the type of Voluntary Winding-Up to which they relate. No registration fees are payable to the Registrar: s. 130(4)(c) Companies Act 1967.

Some forms which are stipulated for Compulsory Winding-Up in the Rules are included because they serve equally well for a Voluntary Liquidation.

1. *Declaration of Solvency*
s.283 (*Members*) *Form*
WUR 108 (*J*)*108* (*R*)

............number of company

form No. WUR 108

no filing fee payable

THE COMPANIES ACTS 1948 To 1976

members' voluntary winding-up

name of company

....

.... Limited

declaration of solvency (a)

embodying a statement of assets and liabilities

WE .... of ....

....

.... of ....

....

.... of ....

....

.... of ....

....

being all (b) / the majority of the Directors of............................ Limited

DO SOLEMNLY AND SINCERELY DECLARE that we have made a full enquiry into the affairs of this Company, and that, having so done, we have formed the opinion that this Company will be able to pay its debts in full within a period of (c)................. months, from the commencement of the winding-up, and we append a statement of the Company's assets and liabilities as at .... 19...... being the latest practicable date before the making of this Declaration, AND WE MAKE THIS SOLEMN DECLARATION conscientiously believing the same to be true, and by virtue of the provisions of the Statutory Declarations Act 1835.

DECLARED at ....

....

the..........day of...........19...... ....

before me

....

A Commissioner for Oaths

[Notary Public] [Justice of the Peace] (b) ....

NOTES:

(a) This Declaration is effective ONLY (1) if it is made within the five weeks immediately preceding the date of the passing of the Resolution for winding up the Company AND (2) if it is delivered to the Registrar of Companies BEFORE the day on which that Resolution was passed.

(b) Delete as necessary.

(c) Insert the period of months not exceeding twelve.

Declaration of Solvency (continued)

Statement as at..................................19......
showing assets at estimated realisable values and liabilities expected to rank

ASSETS AND LIABILITIES				Estimated to realise or to rank for payment (to nearest £)
ASSETS				£
Balance at Bank				
Cash in Hand				
Marketable Securities				
Bills Receivable				
Trade Debtors				
Loans and Advances				
Unpaid Calls				
Stock in Trade				
Work in Progress				
....				
....				
Freehold Property				
Leasehold Property				
Plant and Machinery				
Furniture, Fittings, Utensils, etc.				
Patents, Trade Marks, etc.				
Investments other than marketable securities				
Other property, viz.:				
....				
....				
....				
Estimated realisable value of Assets .. .. £				
LIABILITIES			£	
Secured on specific assets, viz.:				
....				
Secured by Floating Charge(s)				
Estimated Cost of Liquidation and other expenses including interest accruing until payment of debts in full				
Unsecured Creditors (amounts estimated to rank for payment):		£		
Trade Accounts				
Bills Payable				
Accrued Expenses				
Other Liabilities:				
....				
....				
Contingent Liabilities:				
....				
....				
Estimated Surplus after paying Debts in full .. .. £				

Remarks:

2. *Notice of General Meeting to pass Special Winding-Up Resolution and appoint Liquidator*
s.278(1)(b) (*Members*) *C.A. 71* (*J*)

form No. CA 71

Notice to
members of meeting to pass special resolution to wind up company voluntarily

name of company

....

.... Limited

NOTICE IS HEREBY GIVEN that an Extraordinary General Meeting of the above-named Company will be held at ....

....

on day, the .... day of .... 19 ......

at .... o'clock in the .... noon precisely, for the purpose of considering and, if thought fit, passing the following Resolution as a SPECIAL RESOLUTION:—

"That the Company be wound up voluntarily, and that ....

.... [and] (1) ....

of ....

....

be and he is/they are(2) hereby appointed Liquidator(s)(1) for the purpose of such winding-up."

A Member entitled to attend and vote at the above-mentioned Meeting is entitled to appoint a proxy, who need not be a Member of the Company, to attend and vote instead of him.

Dated 19 ....

By order of the Board ....

.... Secretary

NOTES:
(1) Delete if it does not apply
(2) Delete that which does not apply

3. *Statement of Affairs for Creditors' Meeting*
s.293(3) *(Creditors)* *Specimen*

Specimen Statement of Affairs for Creditors' Meeting

A.B.C. (Builders) Limited

Statement of Affairs December 13st 1979

Assets	£	*Book Value* £	£	*Estimated to Realise* £
Freehold Office Premises	6,500			
Less: Bank Mortgage	6,500	—		—
Plant & Equipment		435		200
Office Furnishings and Equipment		743		400
Motor Vehicles	4,754			
Less: Due on Hire Purchase	2,065	2,689		2,000
Stock & Work in Progress	23,000			
Less: Payments on Account	13,593	9,407		9,500
Stock of Hand	45,948			
Less: Mortgages	8,662	37,286		40,000
Debtors		13,347		12,500
Deposits on Road Bonds		6,129		6,129
Cash in Hand		16		16
Associated Company		4,807		4,807
		£74,859		75,552
Less: Preferential Creditors				
Wages, P.A.Y.E., V.A.T., Rates and Taxation				2,461
Amount available to Unsecured Creditors				73,091
Unsecured Creditors				
Trade & Expense Creditors—as set out in List			50,145	
Unsecured Loan			5,000	
Bank		14,899		
Less: Secured		6,500	8,399	
Associated Company			1,315	
Directors Current Accounts			5,737	
				70,596
Surplus as regards Unsecured Creditors				2,495
Issued Share Capital				5,100
Deficiency as regards Members				£2,605

Note: These figures are subject to Costs of Realisation and Liquidation

4. *Notice to Members of General Meeting to pass Extraordinary Winding-Up Resolution and appoint Liquidator*
s.278I(1)(c) *(Creditors)* *Specimen*

A.B.C. Limited

NOTICE IS HEREBY GIVEN that an extraordinary general meeting of A.B.C. Limited will be held

at ....

on..

at ....

for the purpose of considering and, if thought fit, passing the following extraordinary resolution:

(i) That it has been proved to the satisfaction of this meeting that the Company cannot by reason of its liabilities continue its business.
(ii) That it is advisable to wind up the Company.
(iii) That the Company be wound up voluntarily.
(iv) That be nominated as Liquidator for the purpose of such Winding-Up.

Dated ....

By Order of the Board

....

Secretary

NOTE: Each member entitled to attend and vote is entitled to appoint a proxy to attend and vote instead of him. A proxy need not be a member.

Note: Fourteen clear days' notice required.
s.133(1)(b) subject to waiver by 95%
s.133(3)(b)

5A. *Notice to Creditors of their First Meeting*
s.293(1) *(Creditors)* *C.A.76 (J)*

form No. CA 76

Notice of
meeting of creditors (1)

name of company

....

.... Limited

NOTICE IS HEREBY GIVEN, pursuant to section 293 of the Companies Act 1948, that a Meeting of the Creditors of the above-named Company will be held at ....
....
on (2)..............day, the...................day of...................
19......at............o'clock in the..........noon, for the purpose of having a full statement of the position of the Company's affairs, together with a List of the Creditors of the Company and the estimated amount of their claims, laid before them, and for the purpose, if thought fit, of nominating a Liquidator and of appointing a Committee of Inspection. Forms of General and Special Proxy are enclosed herewith. Proxies to be used at the Meeting must be lodged with the Company at its Registered Office at...................................
....
not later than 4 o'clock in the afternoon of the day before the Meeting.
NOTICE IS ALSO GIVEN that, for the purpose of voting, Secured Creditors must (unless they surrender their security) lodge at the said Registered Office of the Company before the Meeting, a statement giving particulars of their Security, the date when it was given, and the value at which it is assessed.

Dated ....19....

By order of the Board of Directors

....

Director or Secretary (3)

NOTES:
(1) This Notice should be sent by post to the Creditors of the Company simultaneously with the sending of the Notices to the Members of the Company.
(2) This date should be the date, or the day next following the date on which the Members' Meeting to pass the Winding-up Resolution is held.
(3) Delete as applicable.

5B. & 5C. *General and Special Proxies to accompany Notice*

Forms 80, 81 (R)
WUR 80, 81 (J)

form Nos. WUR 80 & 81

IMPORTANT—The General **OR** the Special Proxy form should be completed — **BUT NOT BOTH FORMS.**

[Rule 147, The Companies (Winding-up) Rules 1949]

name of company

.... Limited

general proxy

I/We.. of ....
....
a Creditor [or Contributory] hereby appoint (1)...
of..
to be my/our general proxy to vote at the meeting of Creditors [or Contributories] to be held in the above matter on the .... day of .... 19........, or at any adjournment thereof.
Dated .... 19........ Signed (2)..

NOTES:
(1) The person appointed general proxy may, in a voluntary winding-up be the Liquidator or if there is no Liquidator the Chairman of a meeting but not the Official Receiver. The proxy form should be altered accordingly.
(2) If a firm, sign the firm's trading title, and add "by A.B., partner in the said firm." If the appointor is a corporation, then the form of proxy must be under its common seal or under the hand of some officer duly authorised in that behalf, and the fact that the officer is so authorised must be so stated.

special proxy

I/We.. of ....
....
a Creditor [or Contributory] hereby appoint (3)...
of..
as my/our proxy at the meeting of Creditors [or Contributories] to be held on the .... day of .... 19........, or at any adjournment thereof, to vote (4) ....
the resolution numbered .... in the Notice convening.
Dated .... 19........ Signed (2)..

NOTES:
(3) The person appointed proxy may in a voluntary winding-up be the Liquidator or if there is no Liquidator the Chairman of a meeting but not the Official Receiver. The proxy form should be altered accordingly. A Creditor [or Contributory] may give a special proxy to any person to vote at any specified meeting or adjournment thereof on all or any of the following matters:—
(a) For or against the appointment or continuance in office of any specified person as Liquidator or as a member of the Committee of Inspection;
(b) On all questions relating to any matter, other than those above referred to, arising at a specified meeting or adjournment thereof.
(4) Here insert the word "for" or the word "against" as the case may require, and specify the particular resolution.

GENERAL NOTES:
(a) The form of proxy is exempt from stamp duty (Section 339, Companies Act 1948).
(b) The proxy form, when signed, must be lodged by the time and at the address named for that purpose in the Notice convening the meeting at which it is to be used.
(c) The proxy of a Creditor who is blind or incapable of writing may be accepted if such Creditor has attached his signature or mark thereto in the presence of a witness who shall certify below.
(d) This form should be returned from whence it came, and **NOT** to Jordan & Sons Limited.

Certificate to be signed by person filling in proxy for Creditor who is blind or incapable of writing.

I..
Description.. Address ....
....
hereby certify that all insertions in the above proxy have been made at the request and in the presence of ....
before ....he attached h.......... signature [or mark] thereto.
Signature of Witness...
Dated.. 19........

6. *Notice to Creditors of their First Meeting for Publication in Gazette and two Local Newspapers*
s.293(2) *(Creditors)* *C.A. 76a (J)*

form CA 76a
Creditors' Voluntary Winding-up.

notice of meeting of creditors

Pursuant to Section 293 Companies Act, 1948.

Name of Company..**Limited**

Notice is hereby given, pursuant to Section 293 of the Companies Act, 1948, that a meeting of the Creditors of the above-named Company will be held at ....

....

on * .... day, the .... day of .... 19........,

at .... o'clock in the .... noon, for the purpose of having a full statement of the position of the Company's affairs, together with a List of the Creditors of the Company and the estimated amount of their claims, laid before them, and for the purpose, if thought fit, of nominating a Liquidator and of appointing a Committee of Inspection.

Notice is also given that, for the purpose of voting, Secured Creditors must (unless they surrender their security), lodge at the Registered Office of the Company at ....

....

before the Meeting a Statement giving particulars of their security, the date when it was given, and the value at which it is assessed.

Dated this .... day of .... 19........

By Order of the Board of Directors,

....

[Witnessed] [Authenticated for insertion in the "London Gazette"] by

†Director or Secretary.

....

Solicitor,

of ....

For the guidance of Printer, please state name of signatory in BLOCK LETTERS ....

* This date should be the day, or the day next following the day on which the meeting to pass the winding-up resolution is held.
† The signature of the Director or Secretary must be witnessed or authenticated by a Solicitor.

This Notice must also be advertised once at least in two local newspapers circulating in the district where the registered office or principal place or business of the Company is situated.

For insertion of this Notice in the "London Gazette," this form may be returned, after completion, to the Publishers, who are Agents for that purpose.

7. *Members' Special Resolution for Publication in Gazette*
s.279 (*Members*) *C.A. 70A (J)*

........................number of company

form No. CA 70A

THE COMPANIES ACTS 1948 TO 1976

[COPY]

special resolution

pursuant to sections 141(2) and 278(1)(b) of the Companies Act 1948

of ....

.... Limited

Passed ....19......

At an Extraordinary General Meeting of the above-named Company, duly convened, and held at ....

....

on the .... 19......, the following SPECIAL RESOLUTION was duly passed:—

"That the Company be wound up voluntarily, and that ....
.........................[and] (1) ....
of ....
....
....
be and he is/they are(2) hereby appointed Liquidator(s) (1) for the purposes of such winding-up."

Signature (3) ....

Description ....

Authenticated for insertion in
the *London Gazette* by...

Description ....of ....

....

For the guidance of the printer, please state name of person signing at (3) above in BLOCK LETTERS ....

NOTES:
(1) Delete if it does not apply.
(2) Delete that which does not apply.
(3) This form should be signed by the Chairman of the meeting at which the Resolution was passed, or by a Director or the Secretary of the Company and if the Signatory is not a Solicitor or member of a recognised body of Accountants his signature must be authenticated by such a person.
(4) Section 305 of the Companies Act 1948 requires this Notice to be published in the *London Gazette* within 14 days after the appointment of the Liquidator.

..........................number of company

form No. CA 70

no filing fee payable

THE COMPANIES ACTS 1948 TO 1976

[COPY]

special resolution

pursuant to sections 141(2) and 278(1)(b) of the Companies Act 1948

of ....

.... Limited

Passed...19....

At an Extraordinary General Meeting of the members of the above-named Company, duly convened and held at ....

....

on ....19...., the following SPECIAL RESOLUTION was duly passed:—

"That the Company be wound up voluntarily, and that

....

[and] (1) ....

of ....

....

be and he is/they are (2) hereby appointed Liquidator(s) (1) for the purposes of such winding-up."

Signature (3) ....

Description ....

NOTES:
(1) Delete if it does not apply.
(2) Delete that which does not apply.
(3) This form should be signed by the Chairman of the meeting at which the Resolution was passed, or by a Director or the Secretary of the Company.

..........................number of company

form No. CA 73A

THE COMPANIES ACTS 1948 TO 1976

[COPY]

extraordinary resolution

pursuant to sections 141(2), 278(1)(b) and 294 of the Companies Act 1948

of ....

.... Limited

Passed .... 19....

At an Extraordinary General Meeting of the members of the above-named Company, duly convened and held at ....

....

on .... 19...., the following

EXTRAORDINARY RESOLUTION was duly passed:—

"That it has been proved to the satisfaction of this meeting that the Company cannot, by reason of its liabilities, continue its business, and that it is advisable to wind up the same, and accordingly that the Company be wound up voluntarily, and that.............................[and] (1) ....
of ....

....

....

be and he is/they are (2) hereby nominated Liquidator(s) (1) for the purposes of the winding-up.

Signature (3) ....

Description ....

Authenticated for insertion
in the *London Gazette* by ....

Description (4) .... of ....

....

For the guidance of the printer, please state name of person signing Resolution at "(3)" above in BLOCK LETTERS ....

NOTES:
(1) Delete if it does not apply.
(2) Delete that which does not apply.
(3) This form should be signed by the Chairman of the Meeting at which the Resolution was passed, or by a Director or the Secretary of the Company.
(4) This Notice must be signed by, OR attested by, a Solicitor or member of an established body of Accountants or Secretaries, IF the signatory is neither a Solicitor nor a member of any of the above bodies.
(5) Section 305 of the Companies Act 1948 requires this Notice to be published in the *London Gazette* within fourteen days after the appointment of the Liquidator(s).

10. *Members' Extraordinary Resolution for Filing with Registrar*
s.143 *(Creditors)* *C.A. 73 (J)*

..........................number of company

form No. CA 73

no filing fee payable

THE COMPANIES ACTS 1948 TO 1976

[COPY]

extraordinary resolution

pursuant to sections 141(2), 278(1)(3) and 294 of the Companies Act 1948

of..

.... Limited

Passed the .... day of ....19....
At an EXTRAORDINARY GENERAL MEETING of the Members of the above-named Company, duly convened and held at..........................
....
....
on the .... day of ....19....,
the following EXTRAORDINARY RESOLUTION was duly passed:—
"That it has been proved to the satisfaction of this Meeting that the Company cannot, by reason of its liabilities, continue its business, and that it is advisable to wind-up the same, and accordingly that the Company be wound up voluntarily, and that.. [and](1)
....
of ....
....
be and he is/they are (2) hereby nominated Liquidator(s) (1) for the purposes of the winding-up.

Signature (3) ....

Description..

NOTES:
(1) Delete if it does not apply.
(2) Delete that which does not apply.
(3) This form should be signed by the Chairman of the Meeting at which the Resolution was passed, or by a Director or the Secretary of the Company.

11. *Notice of Appointment of Liquidator for Publication in Gazette*

s.305 *(Members and Creditors)* *Form 39E (F)* *39E (J)*

Form No. 39e

THE COMPANIES ACTS 1948 TO 1976

39e

Notice of appointment of liquidator
[Members'] [Creditors']* voluntary winding up

*delete as appropriate

Pursuant to section 305 of the Companies Act 1948

†delete as appropriate

For insertion in the [London][Edinburgh]† Gazette

Name of company

Nature of business

Address of registered office

Liquidator(s) name(s) and address(es)

Date of appointment ______________________

By whom appointed ______________________

Signature(s) ______________ Dated ______________

______________________(Liquidator(s))

Attested by ______________

Description ______________________

12. *Notice of Appointment of Liquidator for Filing with Registrar*
s.305 *(Members)* *Form 39C (F)*
39C (J)

Form No. 39c

G

THE COMPANIES ACTS 1948 TO 1976

Members' voluntary winding up
Notice of appointment of liquidator

39c

Pursuant to section 305 of the Companies Act 1948

Please do not write in this binding margin

Please complete legibly, preferably in black type, or bold block lettering

To the Registrar of Companies

For official use

Company number

Name of company

Limited*

*delete if inappropriate

Nature of business

†delete as appropriate

[I][we]† hereby give you notice that [I][we]† have been appointed liquidator(s) of the above named company

Name(s) of Liquidator(s)	Address(es)

‡State how appointed, whether by resolution of the company, or by the court, and adapt if necessary. See sections 237 & 304 of the Companies Act 1948

The appointment as liquidator(s) was by‡: ______

§To be signed by the liquidator or, if more than one, by each one

Signature(s)§ of Liquidator(s)	Date

Presentor's name, address and reference (if any):

For official use
Liquidation section
Post room

Time critical reference

13. *Notice of Appointment of Liquidator for Filing with Registrar*
s.305 *(Creditors)* *Form 39D (F)*
39D (J)

Form No. 39d

G

THE COMPANIES ACTS 1948 TO 1976

Creditors' voluntary winding up
Notice of appointment of liquidator

Pursuant to section 305 of the Companies Act 1948

39d

Please do not write in this binding margin

Please complete legibly, preferably in black type, or bold block lettering

To the Registrar of Companies

For official use

Company number

Name of company

Limited*

*delete if inappropriate

Nature of business

†delete as appropriate

[I][we]† hereby give you notice that [I][we]† have been appointed liquidator(s) of the above-named company.

Name(s) of Liquidator(s)	Address(es)

§State how appointed, whether by the creditors of the company or by the court. See sections 237 & 304 of the Companies Act 1948

The appointment as liquidator(s) was† by§ ______________________________

______________________________ on ______________ 19______

‡To be signed by each liquidator if more than one

Signature(s)‡ of Liquidator(s)	Date

Presentor's name, address and reference (if any):

For official use
Liquidation section
Post room

Time critical reference

14. *Letter to Creditors to submit Details of Claims (enclosing Notice to Claim)*

(*Members and Creditors*) *Specimen*

To all Creditors

Re: A.B.C. (Builders) Limited

In Voluntary Liquidation

I have to inform you that at a Meeting of Creditors held on the 1st January 1971, I was appointed Liquidator of the above Company, together with a Committee of Inspection consisting of:—

....

....

....

....

A copy of the Statement of Affairs and List of Creditors issued at the Meeting of Creditors is enclosed for your information, together with formal Notice to Claim. A Statement of your Account should be forwarded to me at your earliest convenience.

Yours faithfully,
for and on behalf of
A.B.C. (Builders) Limited

....

Liquidator

15A. *Notice to Creditors to Claim for posting to Creditors*
ss.316, 317 (*Members and Creditors*) *C.A. 74 (J)*
R.106

form No. CA 74

Notice to
creditors to send in particulars of debts or claims

name of company

....

.... Limited
(in voluntary liquidation)

NOTICE is hereby given that the Creditors of the above-named Company are required on or before the .... day of .... 19........ to send in their names and addresses, with particulars of their Debts or Claims, and the names and addresses of their Solicitors (if any), to the undersigned ....

....

of ....

....

the Liquidator(s) of the said Company, and, if so required by notice in writing by the said Liquidator(s), are by their Solicitors or personally to come in and prove their said Debts or Claims at such time and place as shall be specified in such notice, or in default thereof they will be excluded from the benefit of any distribution made before such debts are proved.* [This notice is purely formal and all known Creditors have been, or will be, paid in full.]

Dated..19..........

....

....

Signature(s) of Liquidator(s)

To ....

....

*Please delete if this does not apply

15B. *Notice to Creditors to claim, Publication in Gazette, Publication in a Local Newspaper*
ss.316, 317, R.106 *(Members and Creditors)* *C.A. 74A (J)*

form No. CA 74A

gazette notice to creditors to send in claims

name of company

....

.... Limited
(in voluntary liquidation)

NOTICE is hereby given that the Creditors of the above-named Company are required, on or before the .... day of .... 19 , to send their names and addresses, with particulars of their debts or claims, and the names and addresses of their Solicitors (if any), to the undersigned,

....

of ....

....

the Liquidator(s) of the said Company: and, if so required by notice in writing by the said Liquidator(s), are, by their Solicitors or personally, to come in and prove their said debts or claims at such time and place as shall be specified in such notice, or in default thereof they will be excluded from the benefit of any distribution made before such debts are proved. (1) This notice is purely formal and all known Creditors have been, or will be, paid in full.

Dated .... 19 ....

....

....

Signature(s) of Liquidator(s)

Authenticated for insertion in the *London Gazette* by (2) ....

Description .... of ....

....

For the guidance of the printer please print below the name(s) of the Liquidator(s) in BLOCK LETTERS

....

NOTES:
(1) The sentence next following should be deleted if it does not apply.
(2) The signature(s) of the Liquidator(s) must be authenticated by a Solicitor or a member of an established body of Accountants or Secretaries.

form No. CA 79

Notice to

creditors to come in and prove debts or claims

name of company

....

....Limited

(in voluntary liquidation)

NOTICE IS HEREBY GIVEN that the Creditors of the above-named Company are required on or before the..day of..19.... by their Solicitors or personally at the offices of the undersigned...............................

....

of ....

the Liquidator(s) of the said Company, to come in and prove their said Debts or Claims and to establish their title (if any) to priority under Section 319 of the Companies Act 1948, or in default thereof they will be excluded from the benefit of any distribution made before such Debts are proved, or from objecting to such distribution.

Dated..19....

....

....

Signature(s) of Liquidator(s)

15D. *Notice to Creditors to come in and Prove for Publication in Gazette, Publication in a Local Newspaper (Members and Creditors)* *C.A. 79A (J)*

form No. CA 79A

Notice to **creditors to come in and prove debts or claims**

name of company

....

.... Limited
(in voluntary liquidation)

NOTICE IS HEREBY GIVEN that the Creditors of the above-named Company are required on or before the .... day of ....
19.......... by their Solicitors or personally at the offices of the undersigned

....

....

of ....

....

the Liquidator(s) of the said Company, to come in and prove their said Debts or Claims and to establish their title (if any) to priority under Section 319 of the Companies Act 1948, or in default thereof they will be excluded from the benefit of any distribution made before such Debts are proved, or from objecting to such distribution.

Dated...19..........

....

....

(1) Signature(s) of Liquidator(s)

(1) Authenticated for insertion in the *London Gazette* by..

(2) Description.. of ....

....

For the guidance of the printer please print below the name(s) of the Liquidator(s) in

BLOCK LETTERS ....

NOTES: (1) The signature(s) of the Liquidator(s) must be authenticated by (2) a Solicitor or a member of an established body of Accountants or Secretaries.

16A. *Proof of Debt* (*Sworn*) (*General Form*)
R.94 (*Members and Creditors*) *Form 59* (*R*) *WUR 59A* (*J*)

form No. WUR 59A

[Rule 94 The Companies (Winding-up) Rules 1949]

proof of debt
general form voluntary liquidation

name of company

....
.... Limited
(in voluntary liquidation)

Name and address of Liquidator
to whom this form should be sent:—..
of ....
I [insert full name of Deponent]...
Address ....
.... Occupation ....
MAKE OATH and say: (1) THAT I am [in the employ] [a Director] [the Secretary] (2) of the undermentioned Creditor, and that I am duly authorised by such Creditor to make this Affidavit, and that it is within my own knowledge that the debt hereinafter deposed to was incurred and for the consideration stated, and that such debt, to the best of my knowledge and belief, still remains unpaid and unsatisfied.
THAT the above-named company was, at the date of the resolution for winding-up the same, viz.,...19...., and still is justly and truly indebted to (3)...
....
in the sum of..........................pounds and..........pence for (4)
....
....
....
as shown by the account endorsed hereon [or hereto annexed marked 'A'] for which sum or any part thereof I say that I have not nor hath (5).............
.... or any person by (6).............. order to my knowledge and belief for (6)..............use had or received any manner of satisfaction or security whatsoever, save and except the following (7)

Date	Drawer	Acceptor	Amount	Due date
			£	

SWORN by the above-named
....
at ....
this........ day of ....19......   ....
before me   Signature of Deponent
....
(A Commissioner for Oaths)

ADMITTED			
To vote for	Date	To rank for dividend for	Date
£		£	

Signature of
Liquidator ....

Signature of
Liquidator ....

NOTES:
(1) If proof made by Creditor in person, strike out whole paragraph.
(2) Strike out whichever are inapplicable.
(3) Insert "me, and to C.D. and E.F., my co-partners in trade (if any)," or if by clerk or agent insert name, address and description of principal.
(4) State consideration [as goods sold and delivered by me (and my said partner to the company between the dates of [or moneys advanced by me in respect of the undermentioned bill of exchange] or, as the case may be].
(5) "My said partners or any of them" or "the above-named Creditor" (as the case may be).
(6) "My" or "our" or "their" or "his" (as the case may be).
(7) **Here state the particulars of all securities held, and, where the securities are on the property of the Company, assess the value of the same, and if any bills or other negotiable securities be held specify them in the schedule below. N.B. Bills of Exchange or other negotiable securities must be produced before the proof can be admitted.**

NOTE: The proof cannot be admitted for voting at the first meeting unless it is properly completed and lodged with the Liquidator before the time named in the Notice convening the meeting.

16B. *Proof of Debt (Unsworn) (General Form)*
R.94 *(Members and Creditors)* *Form 59A (R)*

Rule 9

No. 59A (Rule 94)

PROOF OF DEBT (UNSWORN) GENERAL FORM

(Title)

Date of [Winding-up Order] [Resolution for Voluntary winding-up].

Name of Creditor ____________________

____

Address of Creditor ____________________

____

Total Amount of Claim as at Date of Winding-Up Order £

Particulars of how Debt(s) arose and Date(s) incurred (use space overleaf if necessary) ____________________

Particulars of any Security held ____________________

Value of Security £

Please attach any documentary evidence of claim.

N.B.—Bills or other negotiable securities must be produced before the proof can be admitted.

Signature of creditor or person signing on his behalf ____________________

Name in block letters ____________________

Position with or relationship to creditor ____________________

[Admitted to vote for	Admitted to rank for dividend for
£	£
the day of 19 .	this day of 19 .
Official Receiver.]	Liquidator

17. *Notice of Rejection of Proof of Debt*
R.107 (*Members and Creditors*) *Form 61* (*R*) *WUR 61* (*J*)

form No. WUR 61
(Rule 107 The Companies (Winding-up) Rules 1949)

Notice of **rejection of proof of debt**

name of company

....

.... Limited
(in voluntary liquidation)

TAKE NOTICE that, as Liquidator(s) of the above-named Company, I/we have this day rejected your claim against the Company [*to the extent of £..] on the following grounds:—

....

....

....

....

....

....

AND FURTHER TAKE NOTICE that, subject to the power of the Court to extend the time, no application to reverse or vary my decision in rejecting your proof will be entertained after the expiration of .... days from this date.

Dated..19............

....

....

Signature(s) of Liquidator(s)

Address..

....

NOTE:
*If proof is wholly rejected strike out the words in brackets.

To..

of..

....

18. *Liquidator's Statement under s.342 when Liquidation continues for more than one year*

s.342	(*Members and*	*Form 92* (*R*)
R.196–198	*Creditors*)	WUR 92 (*J*)

form No. WUR 92

no filing fee payable

..................number of company

THE COMPANIES (WINDING-UP RULES) 1949

rules 197, 198 and 201

[re..Limited

This is the exhibit marked B referred to in the affidavit of........

....

sworn before me this.............day of.............19....

..................................A Commissioner for Oaths)

name of company

....Limited

statement of receipts and payments and general directions as to statements

Size of sheets

(1) Every statement must be on sheets 11¾ inches by 16½ inches.

Form and contents of statement

(2) Every statement must contain a detailed account of all the liquidator's realizations and disbursements in respect of the Company. The statement of realizations should contain a record of all receipts derived from assets existing at the date of the winding-up resolution and subsequently realized, including balance in bank, book debts and calls collected, property sold, etc.: and the account of disbursements should contain all payments for costs and charges, or to creditors or contributories. Where property has been realized, the gross proceeds of sale must be entered under realizations, and the necessary payments incidental to sales must be entered as disbursements. These accounts should not contain payments into the Companies Liquidation Account (except unclaimed dividends, see paragraph (5)) or payments into or out of bank, or temporary investments by the liquidator, or the proceeds of such investments when realized, which should be shewn separately:—

(a) by means of the bank pass sheets;

(b) by a separate detailed statement of moneys invested by the liquidator, and investments realized.

Interest allowed or charged by the bank, bank commission, etc., and profit or loss upon the realization of temporary investments, should, however, be inserted in the accounts of realizations or disbursements, as the case may be. Each receipt and payment must be entered in the account in such a manner as sufficiently to explain its nature. The receipts and payments must severally be added up at the foot of each sheet, *and the totals carried forward from one account to another without any intermediate balance, so that the gross totals shall represent the total amounts received and paid by the liquidator respectively.*

Trading account

(3) When the liquidator carries on a business, a trading account must be forwarded as a distinct account, and the totals of receipts and payments on the trading account must alone be set out in the statement.

Dividends, etc.

(4) When dividends or instalments of compositions are paid to creditors, or a return of surplus assets is made to contributories, the total amount of each dividend, or instalment of composition, or return to contributories, actually paid, must be entered in the statement of disbursements as one sum; and the liquidator must forward separate accounts shewing in lists the amount of the claim of each creditor, and the amount of dividend or composition payable to each creditor, and of surplus assets payable to each contributory, distinguishing in each list the dividends or instalments of composition and shares of surplus assets actually paid, and those remaining unclaimed. Each list must be on sheets 11¾ inches by 8¼ inches.

(5) When unclaimed, dividends, instalments of compositions, or returns of surplus assets are paid into the Companies Liquidation Account the total amount so paid in should be entered in the statement of disbursements as one sum.

(6) Credit should not be taken in the statement of disbursements for any amount in respect of liquidator's remuneration unless it has been duly allowed by resolution of the Committee of Inspection, or of the creditors, or of the Company in general meeting, or by order of Court, as the case may require.

---

liquidators' statement of account

pursuant to section 342 of the Companies Act 1948

name of company

.... Limited

Nature of proceedings (whether a members' or creditors' voluntary winding-up or a winding-up under the supervision of the Court)....................

Date of commencement of winding-up....................................

Date to which statement is brought down...............................

Name and address of liquidator...

....

NOTE: *This statement is required in DUPLICATE, and must be accompanied by an affidavit verifying the same (form WUR 93).

liquidator's statement of account

pursuant to section 342 of the Companies Act 1948

REALIZATIONS			
Date	Of whom received	Nature of assets realized	Amount
			£
		Brought forward ..	

DISBURSEMENTS			
Date	To whom paid	Nature of disbursements	Amount
			£
		Brought forward ..	

analysis of balance

		£
Total Realizations		
Total Disbursements		
Balance .. £		
The Balance is made up as follows:		£
1. Cash in hands of liquidator		
2. Total payments into bank, including balance at date of commencement of winding-up (*as per bank book*)	£	
Total withdrawals from bank		
Balance at bank		
3. Amount in Companies Liquidation Account		
4.* Amounts invested by liquidator ..	£	
Less Amounts realised from same ..		
Balance ..		
Total Balance as shewn above .. £		

NOTE: Full details of stocks purchased for investment and realization thereof should be given in a separate statement

*The investment or deposit of money by the liquidator does not withdraw it from the operation of section 343 of the Companies Act 1948, and any such investments representing money held for six months or upwards must be realized and paid into the Companies Liquidation Account, except in the case of investments in Government securites the transfer of which to the control of the Board of Trade will be accepted as a sufficient compliance with the terms of the section.

---

note—the liquidator should also state—

(1) The amount of the estimated assets and liabilities at the date of the commencement of the winding-up:

	£
Assets (after deducting amounts charged to secured creditors and debenture holders)	
Liabilities—Secured creditors	
Debenture holders	
Unsecured creditors	

(2) The total amount of the capital paid up at the date of the commencement of the winding-up:

Paid up in cash .. ..

Issued as paid up otherwise than for cash .. ..

(3) **The general description and estimated value of outstanding assets (if any):**

....

....

(4) **The causes which delay the termination of the winding-up:**

....

....

(5) **The period within which the winding-up may probably be completed:**

....

....

19. *Liquidator's Affidavit under s.342*

s.342	*(Members and*	*Form 93 (R)*
R.196–198	*Creditors)*	*WUR 93 (J)*

....number of company

form No. WUR 93

no filing fee payable

affidavit(1)

verifying statement of liquidator's account

under section 342 of the Companies Act 1948 and pursuant to rules 197, 198 and 201 of the Companies (Winding-up) Rules 1949

name of company

....

.... Limited

I, ...

of ....

....

the Liquidator of the above-named Company, make oath and say:—

That (2)*the Account hereunto annexed, marked "B", contains a full and true account of my Receipts and Payments in the winding-up of the above-named Company*

from the .... day of .... 19..........

to the .... day of .... 19..........,

inclusive, (2)*and that* I have not, nor has any other person by my order or for my use during such period, received or paid any moneys on account of the said Company, (2)*other than and except the items mentioned and specified in the said Account.*

I further say that the particulars given in the annexed form 92, marked "B", with respect to the proceedings in and position of the liquidation, are true to the best of my knowledge and belief.

SWORN at ....

....

this .... day of .... 19..........

....

before me

....

A Commissioner for Oaths or Notary Public

NOTES:
(1) This Affidavit is **not** required in duplicate, but it must in every case be accompanied by a Statement on Form WUR 92 which has to be in duplicate.
(2) If no Receipts or Payments, strike out the words in italics.

..........................number of company

form No. WUR 94

no filing fee payable

liquidator's trading account

under section 342 of the Companies Act 1948, and pursuant to rules 197 and 201 of the Companies (Winding-up) Rules 1949

name of company

....

.... Limited

Name of Liquidator ....

the Liquidator of the above-named Company in account with the Estate.
This account is required in duplicate in addition to form No. WUR 92.

receipts

Dr.

Date		£
....	....	....
....	....	....
	Total £	

payments

Cr.

Date		£
....	....	....
....	....	....
	Total £	

Dated....................19.... Liquidator..........................

..............................number of company

form No. WUR 95

list of dividends or composition

under section 342 of the Companies Act 1948, and pursuant to rules 197 and 201 of the Companies (Winding-up) Rules 1949

name of company

....

.... Limited

I HEREBY CERTIFY that a Dividend (or Composition) of..................in the £ was declared payable on and after the................day of............ 19.... and that the Creditors whose names are set forth below are entitled to the amounts set opposite their respective names, and have been paid such amounts except in the cases specified as unclaimed.

Dated..19....

....Liquidator

To the Board of Trade

Surname	Christian names	Amount of Proof	Amount of Dividend (or Composition)	
			Paid	Unclaimed
		£	£	£
....	....	....	....	....
....	....	....	....	....
	Total £			

This list is required in duplicate.

..........................number of company

form No. WUR 96

list of amounts paid or payable to contributories

under section 342 of the Companies Act 1948, and pursuant to rules 197 and 201 of the Companies (Winding-up) Rules 1949

name of company

....

.... Limited

I HEREBY CERTIFY that a Return of Surplus Assets was declared payable to Contributories on and after the .... day of................. 19...., at the rate of..................per share, and that the Contributories whose names are set forth below are entitled to the amounts set opposite their respective names, and have been paid such amounts except in the cases specified as unclaimed.

Dated......................................19....

.....................................Liquidator

To the Board of Trade

Surname	Christian names	No. of shares	Amount returned on shares	
			Paid	Unclaimed
			£	£
....	....	....	....	....
....	....	....	....	....
	Totals			

This list is required in duplicate.

21. *Notice of Members' Meeting when Liquidation continues for more than One Year*
s.289 (*Members and* *C.A. 98 (J)*
s.299 *Creditors*)

form No. CA 98

THE COMPANIES ACTS 1948 TO 1967

notice to members of meeting when winding-up continues for more than a year

name of company

....

....Limited

(members' voluntary winding-up)

NOTICE IS HEREBY GIVEN pursuant to section 289(1) of the Companies Act 1948, that a General Meeting of the Members of the above-named Company will be held at..

....

on ....day, the ....day of ....19...., at..............o'clock in the........noon precisely, to receive the account of the Liquidator(s) acts and dealings, and of the conduct of the winding-up, during the twelve months ended the.............day of.................. 19...., and to hear any explanation that may be given by the Liquidator(s).

Any Member entitled to attend and vote at the above-mentioned Meeting is entitled to appoint a proxy, who need not be a member of the Company to attend and vote instead of him.

Dated.......................................19....

....

....

Signature(s) of Liquidator(s)

22. *Notice of Creditors' Meeting when Liquidation continues for more than One Year*
s.299 *(Creditors)* *Specimen*

THE COMPANIES ACTS 1948 TO 1967

A.B.C. Limited in voluntary liquidation, creditors winding-up

I hereby give you notice that pursuant to s.299 of the Companies Act 1948 a Meeting of the Creditors of the Company will be held

at ....

on ....

at ....

when I shall lay before the Meeting an account of my acts and dealings and of the conduct of the winding-up of the Company during the year ending .... (including reference to proxies and forms of proxy as in specimens 5, 5A and 5B).

....
Liquidator

Note: Seven days' notice required and publication in *Gazette* and one local paper.

23. *Liquidator's Final Account and Return of Final Meetings*
s.290 (*Members*) Form *110* (*R*)
R.182 *WUR 110, 111* (*J*)

..........................number of company

form No. WUR 111

[Form WUR 110 attached]

no filing fee payable

THE COMPANIES ACTS 1948 TO 1976

members' voluntary winding-up

return of final winding-up meeting

pursuant to section 290 of the Companies Act 1948
To the Registrar of Companies

name of company

....

.... Limited

I (or We)...

of ....

....

being the liquidator(s) of the above-named company have to inform you that a general meeting of the company was duly (1) held on / summoned for ....19..
pursuant to section 290 of the Companies Act 1948 for the purpose of having an account (2) (a copy of which is attached hereto) laid before it showing how the winding-up of the company has been conducted, and the property of the company has been disposed of, and that (1) the same was done accordingly. / no quorum was present at the meeting.

Signature(s) (3)

....

....

Dated.......................................19....

NOTES:
(1) Strike out that which does not apply.
(2) The copy account attached to this Return must ALSO be authenticated by the written signature(s) of the Liquidator(s).
(3) To be signed by each Liquidator if more than one.

liquidator's statement of account (members') (a) (creditors') voluntary winding-up

pursuant to sections 290 and 300 of the Companies Act 1948

statement showing how the winding-up has been conducted and the

name of company

....

.... Limited (in liquidation)

	Statement of assets and liabilities	Receipts
RECEIPTS	£	£
Cash in Bank		
Cash in hand		
Marketable securities		
Sundry debtors		
Stock in trade		
Work in progress		
Freehold property		
Leasehold property		
Plant and machinery		
Furniture, fittings, utensils, etc		
Patents, trade marks, etc.		
Investments other than marketable securities ..		
Surplus from securities		
Unpaid calls at commencement of winding-up		
Amounts received from calls on contributories made in the winding-up		
Receipts per trading account		
Other property, viz.:		
....		
....		
....		
....		
£		
	£	
Less—		
Payments to redeem securities		
Costs of execution		
Payments per trading account		
Net Realisations	£	

(1) Assets, including .... shown in the statement of assets and liabilities and estimated to be of the value of £............... have proved to be unrealisable.

(2) State amount paid into the Companies Liquidation Account in respect of:
- (a) unclaimed dividends payable to creditors in the winding-up .. .. £
- (b) other unclaimed distributions in the winding-up .. .. .. £
- (c) moneys held by the company in trust in respect of dividends or other sums due before the commencement of the winding-up to any person as a member of the company .. .. £

(3) Add here any special remarks the liquidator(s) think(s) desirable:

..............................number of company

form No. WUR 110

(Rule 182, The Companies
(Winding-up) Rules 1949)

property of the company has been disposed of

from ....19.... (commencement of winding-up)
to ....19.... (close of winding-up)

	Payments
Costs of solicitor to liquidator	£
Other law costs	
Liquidator's remuneration:	
(Where applicable) ......% on £............ realised .. £	
......% on £............ distributed .. £	
By whom fixed..	
Auctioneer's and valuer's charges	
Costs of possession and maintenance of estate	
Costs of notices in *Gazette* and local papers	
Incidental outlay	
Total costs and charges .. .. £	
(i) Debenture holders:	
Payment of £............ per £...... debenture £	
Payment of £............ per £...... debenture £	
Payment of £............ per £...... debenture £	
(ii) Creditors:	
............(b) Preferential .. .. .. £	
............(b) Unsecured:	
Dividend(s) of........p in £ on £............ £	
(The estimate of amount expected to rank for dividend was £............)	
(iii) Return to contributories:	
........p per £......................(c)share £	
........p per £......................(c)share £	
........p per £......................(c)share £	
£	

Signature(s) of liquidator(s) (d)..
Address(es) ....
....
....
Dated..19....

NOTES:
(a) Strike out that which does not apply.
(b) State number. Preferential creditors need not be separately shown if all creditors have been paid in full.
(c) State nominal value and class of share.
(d) To be signed by each Liquidator if more than one.

24. *Notice to Members of Final Meeting*
s.290 *(Members)* *C.A. 75 (J)*

form No. CA 75

notice to members of final meeting
(members' voluntary winding-up)

name of company

....

.... Limited

(in voluntary liquidation)

NOTICE is hereby given, pursuant to sections 290 and 341(1)(b) of the Companies Act 1948 that a General Meeting of the Members of the above-named Company will be held at...

....

on..........day, the......................day of..................19....,

at.......... o'clock in the ....noon precisely, for the purpose of having an Account laid before them, and to receive the Liquidator(s) report showing how the winding-up of the Company has been conducted and its property disposed of, and of hearing any explanation that may be given by the Liquidator(s); and also of determining by Extraordinary Resolution the manner in which the books, accounts, papers and documents of the Company and of the Liquidator(s) thereof, shall be disposed of.

Note: Any Member entitled to attend and vote at the above-mentioned Meeting is entitled to appoint a proxy to attend and vote instead of him, and such proxy need not also be a Member.

Dated......................................19....

....

....

Signature(s) of the Liquidator(s)

*NOTE:
Section 290 of the Companies Act 1948 requires this Notice to be advertised in the *London Gazette* at least one month before the date of the meeting. (Form CA 75A should be completed).

25. *Notice to Members of Final Meeting for Publication in Gazette*
s.290 (*Members*) *C.A. 75A* (*J*)

form No. CA 75A

notice to members of final meeting
(members' voluntary winding-up)

name of company

....

.... Limited

(in voluntary liquidation)

NOTICE is hereby given, pursuant to sections 290 and 341(1)(b) of the Companies Act 1948 that a General Meeting of the Members of the above-named Company will be held at..

....

on (1)............day, the..............day of...................19....,
at.............. o'clock in the ....noon precisely, for the purpose of having an Account laid before them, and to receive the Liquidator(s) report, showing how the winding up of the Company has been conducted and its property disposed of, and of hearing any explanation that may be given by the Liquidator(s); and also of determining by Extraordinary Resolution the manner in which the books, accounts, papers and documents of the Company and of the Liquidator(s) thereof, shall be disposed of.
Any Member entitled to attend and vote at the above-mentioned Meeting is entitled to appoint a proxy to attend and vote instead of him, and such proxy need not also be a Member.

Dated.......................................19....

....

....

Signature(s) of the Liquidator(s) (2)

Authenticated for insertion in

the *London Gazette* by..

Description.................................... of ....

....

For the guidance of the printer please print below the name(s) of the Liquidator(s) in BLOCK LETTERS

NOTES:
(1) Section 290 of the Companies Act 1948 requires this Notice to be advertised in the *London Gazette* at least one month before the date of the meeting.
(2) The signature(s) of the Liquidator(s) must be authenticated by a Solicitor or a member of an established body of Accountants or Secretaries.

26. *Liquidator's Final Account and Return of Final Meetings*
s.300 *(Creditors)* *Form 110 (R)*
R.182 *WUR 110, 112 (J)*

..........................number of company

form No. WUR 112

[Form WUR 110 attached]

no filing fee payable

THE COMPANIES ACTS 1948 TO 1976

creditors' voluntary winding-up

return of final winding-up meeting

pursuant to section 300 of the Companies Act 1948

To the Registrar of Companies

name of company

....

.... Limited

I (or We)...

of ....

....

being the Liquidator(s) of the above-named company have to inform you—

(1) That a general meeting of this company was duly (a) held on / summoned for the ....19...., pursuant to section 300 of the Companies Act 1948, for the purpose of having an account (b) (a copy of which is attached hereto) laid before it showing how the winding-up of the company has been conducted and the property of the company has been disposed of and that (a) the same was done accordingly. / no quorum was present at the meeting.

(2) That a meeting of the Creditors of this company was duly (a) held on / summoned for the...................19...., pursuant to section 300 of the Companies Act 1948, for the purpose of having the said account laid before it showing how the winding-up of the company has been conducted and the property of the company has been disposed of and that (a) the same was done accordingly. / no quorum was present at the meeting.

Signature(s) (c)

....

....

Dated..............................19....

NOTES:
(a) Strike out that which does not apply.
(b) The copy account attached to this Return must ALSO be authenticated by the written signature(s) of the Liquidator(s).
(c) To be signed by each Liquidator if more than one.

liquidator's statement of account (members') (a) (creditors') voluntary winding-up

pursuant to sections 290 and 300 of the Companies Act 1948

statement showing how the winding-up has been conducted and the

name of company

..............1...

.... Limited (in liquidation)

	Statements of assets and liabilities	Receipts
RECEIPTS	£	£
Cash in bank		
Cash in hand		
Marketable securities		
Sundry debtors		
Stock in trade		
Work in progress		
Freehold property		
Leasehold property		
Plant and machinery		
Furniture, fittings, utensils, etc.		
Patents, trade marks, etc.		
Investments other than marketable securities		
Surplus from securities		
Unpaid calls at commencement of winding-up		
Amounts received from calls on contributories made in the winding-up		
Receipts per trading account		
Other property, viz.:		
....		
....		
....		
....		
£		
Less—	£	
Payments to redeem securities		
Costs of execution		
Payments per trading account		
Net Realisations .. .. £		

(1) Assets, including ....
shown in the statement of assets and liabilities and estimated to be of the value of £.................
have proved to be unrealisable.

(2) State amount paid into the Companies Liquidation Account in respect of:
- (a) unclaimed dividends payable to creditors in the winding-up .. .. £
- (b) other unclaimed distributions in the winding-up .. .. .. £
- (c) moneys held by the company in trust in respect of dividends or other sums due before the commencement of the winding-up to any person as a member of the company .. .. £

(3) Add here any special remarks the liquidator(s) think(s) desirable:

..........................number of company

form No.WUR 110

(Rule 182, The Companies (Winding-up) Rules 1949)

property of the company has been disposed of

from ....19....(commencement of winding-up)
to.................... 19.... (close of winding-up)

	Payments
Costs of solicitor to liquidator	£
Other law costs	
Liquidator's remuneration:	
(Where).....% on £............. realised .. £	
(applicable).....% on £........... distributed .. £	
By whom fixed...	
Auctioneer's and valuer's charges	
Costs of possession and maintenance of estate	
Costs of notices in *Gazette* and local papers	
Incidental outlay	
Total costs and charges .. .. £	
(i) Payment of £........... per £...... debenture £	
Payment of £........... per £...... debenture £	
Payment of £........... per £...... debenture £	
(ii) Creditors:	
............(b) Preferential .. .. .. £	
............(b) Unsecured:	
Dividend(s) of........p in £ on £........... £	
(The estimate of amount expected to rank for dividend was £..........)	
(iii) Return to contributories:	
........p per £......................(c)share £	
........p per £......................(c)share £	
........p per £......................(c)share £	
£	

Signature(s) of liquidator(s) (d)......................................
Address(es) ....
....
....
Dated..............................19....

NOTES:
(a) Strike out that which does not apply.
(b) State number. Preferential creditors need not be separately shown if all creditors have been paid in full.
(c) State nominal value and class of share.
(d) To be signed by each Liquidator if more than one.

27. *Notice to Creditors of Final Meeting for Publication in Gazette s.300 (Creditors) C.A. 77A (J)*

form No. CA 77A

Notice to **creditors of final meeting**

(creditors' voluntary winding-up)

name of company

....

.... Limited

(in voluntary liquidation)

NOTICE is hereby given pursuant to sections 300 and 341 (1) (b) of the Companies Act 1948 that a Meeting of the Creditors of the above-named Company will be held at

....

....

on (1) .... day, the .... day of .... 19 ....

at .... o'clock in the .... noon precisely, for the purpose of having an Account laid before them, and to receive the report of the Liquidator(s) showing how the winding-up of the Company has been conducted and its property disposed of, and of hearing any explanation that may be given by the Liquidator(s) (2) [and also of determining the manner in which the books, accounts, papers and documents of the Company, and of the Liquidator(s) therefore, shall be disposed of]. Proxies to be used at the Meeting must be lodged with the Liquidator(s) at ....

....

not later than 4 o'clock in the afternoon of the day before the Meeting.

....

....

(3) Signature(s) of the Liquidator(s)

Dated .... 19 ....

Authenticated for insertion
in the *London Gazette* by (3)

Description (4) .... of ....

....

For the guidance of the printer please print below the name(s) of the Liquidator(s) in

BLOCK LETTERS ....

NOTES:
(1) Section 300 of the Companies Act 1948 requires this Notice to be advertised in the *London Gazette* at least one month before the date of the Meeting.
(2) If the Committee of Inspection has passed a Resolution as to the disposal of books, accounts and documents, delete the words in square brackets.
(3) The signature(s) of the Liquidator(s) must be authenticated (4) by a Solicitor or member of an established body of Accountants or Secretaries.

28. *Notice to Members of Final Meeting in Creditors' Winding-Up, for Publication in Gazette*
s.300 (*Creditors*) *C.A. 78A (J)*

form No. CA 78A

Notice to
members of final meeting
(creditors' voluntary winding-up)

name of company

....
.... Limited
(in voluntary liquidation)

NOTICE is hereby given pursuant to section 300 of the Companies Act 1948 that a General Meeting of the above-named Company will be held at........
....
....
on (1)...............day, the............... day of ....19....
at............... o'clock in the ....noon precisely, for the purpose of having an Account laid before them, and to receive the report of the Liquidator(s) showing how the winding-up of the Company has been conducted and its property disposed of, and of hearing any explanation that may be given by the Liquidator(s).
Any Member entitled to attend and vote is entitled to appoint a proxy to attend and vote instead of him, and such proxy need not also be a Member.

....
....
(2) Signature(s) of the Liquidator(s)

Dated...................................19....

Authenticated for insertion
in the *London Gazette* by (2)..................................

Description (3) ....of.........................
....

For the guidance of the printer please print below the name(s) of the Liquidator(s) in BLOCK LETTERS..................................

NOTES:
(1) Section 300 of the Companies Act 1948 requires this Notice to be advertised in the *London Gazette* at least one month before the date of the Meeting.
(2) The signature(s) of the Liquidator(s) must be authenticated (3) by a Solicitor or member of an established body of Accountants or Secretaries.

29. *Extraordinary Resolution for Disposal of Books and Papers for Filing with Registrar*
s.341 *(Members)* *51A (J)*

..........................number of company

form No. 51A

no filing fee payable

THE COMPANIES ACTS 1948 TO 1967

[COPY]

extraordinary resolution

pursuant to section 141(1) of the Companies Act 1948

of...

.... Limited

Passed the..............day of......................... 19....

At an Extraordinary General Meeting of the members of the above-named company, duly convened and held at (1).................................

....

....

on the......................day of..............................19....

the following EXTRAORDINARY RESOLUTION was duly passed:

"That all the books, accounts, papers and documents of the Company and of the Liquidator be retained by the Liquidator for a period of (2)............... from the dissolution of the Company, after which they shall be destroyed by him."

....

.Signature of Liquidator

NOTES:
(1) Insert the full address of the place where the meeting was held.
(2) Complete as appropriate.

30. *Minutes of Creditors' Final Meeting*
s.300 (*Creditors*) *Specimen*

minutes of final meeting of the creditors of A.B.C. Limited

held under s.300 Companies Act 1948

at ....

....

Present... Liquidator. Chairman.

and the following Creditors.

....

....

....

Resolved

(1) That the final accounts of the Liquidator as laid before the meeting be approved.
(2) That the Liquidator's remuneration be fixed at % on realisations and % on distributions.
(3) That Messrs. and Company (the Liquidator's professional firm) be paid a fee of £ for accountancy and taxation services.
(4) That the Liquidator be empowered to destroy the books and papers of the Company three months after dissolution.

....

Signature of Liquidator

31. *Statement of Assets and Liabilities where Liquidator considers Debts will not be paid within the Period stated in Declaration of Solvency*
s.288 (*Members*) *Form 109* (*R*)
WUR 109 (*J*)

form No. WUR 109

THE COMPANIES ACTS 1948 TO 1967

Form of

statement of assets and liabilities

To be submitted to a Meeting of Creditors pursuant to section 288 of the Companies Act 1948, by the Liquidator in a Members' Voluntary Winding-up if he is of the opinion that the Company is unable to pay its debts in full **within the period stated in the**

Declaration of Solvency, viz........................*months from the commencement of the Winding-up.

name of company

....

.... Limited

(in liquidation)

Statement as at.................................. 19....
showing Assets at estimated realisable values and Liabilities expected to rank.

Date of Commencement of winding-up................19 ....

LIQUIDATOR'S REMARKS

in particular the Liquidator should draw attention to any item where after taking his receipts and payments into account there is a substantial difference between his estimate and the directors' estimate in the statement annexed to the Declaration of Solvency.

*Insert period shown in the Declaration of Solvency.

name of company

....

....Limited (in liquidation)

statement as at.................... 19.... showing assets at estimated realisable values and liabilities expected to rank.

(date of commencement of winding-up............ 19....

	Estimated realisable values £
Assets not specifically pledged:	
Balance at Bank	
Cash in Hand	
Marketable securities	
Bills Receivable	
Trade Debtors	
Loans and Advances	
Unpaid Calls	
Stock in Trade	
Work in Progress	
....	
....	
Freehold Property	
Leasehold Property	
Plant and Machinery	
Furniture, Fittings, Utensils, etc.	
Patents, Trade Marks, etc.	
Investments other than marketable securities	
Other property, viz. :—	
....	
....	

	(a) Estimated Realisable Values	(b) Due to secured creditors	(c) Deficiency ranking as unsecured (*see* next page)	Surplus carried to last column
Assets specifically pledged:	£	£	£	£
Freehold property ..				
....				
....				
	£	£	£	£

	Estimated realisable values £
Estimated surplus from Assets specifically pledged ..	
Estimated Total Assets available for Preferential Creditors, Debenture Holders secured by a Floating Charge, and Unsecured Creditors* (carried forward to next page) ..£	

Summary of Gross Assets	(d) £
Gross realisable value of assets specifically pledged ..	
Other Assets	
Gross Assets £	

Estimated Total Assets available for Preferential Creditors, Debenture Holders secured by a Floating Charge, and Unsecured Creditors* (brought forward from preceding page) .. £

(*e*) Gross Liabilities £

Liabilities

(to be deducted from surplus or added to deficiency as the case may be)

Secured Creditors to extent to which claims are estimated to be covered by Assets specifically pledged (item (*a*) or (*b*) on preceding page whichever is the less). [Insert in "Gross Liabilities" column only.] —

Preferential Creditors .. ..

Estimated balance of assets available for Debenture Holders secured by a floating charge and Unsecured Creditors* .. .. £

Debenture Holders secured by a floating charge ..

Estimated **Surplus/Deficiency** as regards Debenture Holders* .. .. £

Unsecured Creditors:— £

Estimated unsecured balance of claims of Creditors partly secured on specific assets, brought from preceding page (*c*) .. .. ..

Trade Accounts .. ..

Bills Payable .. ..

Outstanding Expenses .. .. ..

....

....

Contingent Liabilities (state nature) :—

....

Estimated Surplus/Deficiency as regards Creditors being the difference between :— **Gross Assets,** brought from preceding page (*d*) and **Gross Liabilities,** as per column (*e*) £

£

Issued and Called-up Capital £

..........preference shares of........each..

..........called-up .. .. ..

..........ordinary shares of........each ..

..........called-up .. .. ..

....

....

Estimated Surplus/Deficiency as regards Members* £

* These figures must be read subject to the following notes:—

† (1)(*f*) There is no unpaid capital liable to be called up *or* (*g*) The nominal amount of capital liable to be called up is £ estimated to produce £ which is/is not charged in favour of Debenture Holders.

(2) The estimates are subject to costs of the winding-up and to any surplus or deficiency or trading pending realisation of Assets.

† Strike out (*f*) or (*g*).

32. *Notice of Meeting to receive Form 109 (R) above*
s.288 *(Members)* *C.A.99A (J)*

form No. CA 99A

THE COMPANIES ACTS 1948 TO 1967

Notice of
meeting of creditors in case of insolvency

name of company

....

.... Limited

(in voluntary liquidation)

NOTICE IS HEREBY GIVEN pursuant to section 288 (1) of the Companies Act 1948, that a Meeting of the Creditors of the above-named Company will be held at

....

....

on(1)..................day, the .... day of .... 19..........,

at .... o'clock in the ....noon precisely, for the purpose of laying before the Meeting a Statement of the Assets and Liabilities of the Company.

Proxies to be used at the Meeting must be lodged with ....

....

at ....

in the County of ...., not later than .... o'clock in

the ....noon on the .... day of .... 19..........

Dated this .... day of .... 19..........

Signature(s) of Liquidator(s) (2)

....

....

Authenticated for insertion in
the *London Gazette* by (2)..

Description (3).. of..

....

For the guidance of the Printer, please print below the name(s) of the Liquidator(s)

IN BLOCK LETTERS ....

NOTES:
(1) Rule 129 (1) of The Companies (Winding-up) Rules 1949 requires this Notice to be advertised in the *London Gazette* and in a local paper not less than seven days before the date appointed for the Meeting.
(2) The Signature(s) of the Liquidator(s) must be authenticated (3) by a Solicitor or member of an established body of Accountants or Secretaries.

33. *Notice of Dividend*
R.119(3) *(Creditors)* *Form 65 (R)*

No. 65 (Rule 119(3))

NOTICE OF DIVIDEND

(Title)

Address

Date 19 .

Notice is hereby given that a dividend of p in the £ has been declared in this matter, and that the same may be received at my office, as above, on the day of 19 or any subsequent weekday, except , between the hours of and .

NOTE:

(i) This form must be presented, or returned, to the Liquidator when application for payment is made. Any bills of exchange, promissory notes or other negotiable instruments held by you must be produced.

(ii) If you desire the dividend to be paid to some other person you should sign and lodge with the Liquidator an authority in the prescribed form No. 68.

(iii) If you do not desire to attend personally you must fill up, sign and return the form of authority below, when a dividend payable order will be delivered in accordance with the authority.

(iv) Dividend payable orders lapse if not presented for payment within 3 months of the last day of the month of issue but will be re-issued after that period on application to the Department of Trade and Industry.

The fee payable on re-issue of a payable order is 13p where the order is for £5 or less, and 25p where the order exceeds £5.

(Signed)

Liquidator.

To ....

AUTHORITY

Sir,

Please deliver to *me (us) by post, / the Bearer, Mr. at my (our) risk the Dividend Payable Order for £ being the amount payable to *me / us in respect of the dividend of in the £ on *our / my claim in this matter.

£ .

Creditor's signature

To the Liquidator Date 19

NOTE. The authority should be signed by—

(*a*) the creditor personally, or
(*b*) in the case of a firm, by one of the partners, or
(*c*) in the case of a limited company, by an officer of the company, so described, or
(*d*) in the case of a holder of a general proxy authorised to receive the dividend, by the holder.

(For use when payable order handed to creditor or representative)
Received Payable Order for £ ______ Signed

Date 19

* Strike out words inapplicable.

Form No. 35. (Rule 75.)

DISCLAIMER OF LEASE

(*Title*.)

Pursuant to an Order of the Court dated the day of , 19 ,

I, , the Liquidator of the above-named company, hereby disclaim all interest in the lease dated the day of , 19 , whereby the premises (*a*) were demised to at a rent of £ per annum for a term of

Notice of this disclaimer has been given to

Dated this day of , 19 .

Liquidator.

(*a*) Insert description of the property disclaimed.

Form No. 36. (Rule 75.)

NOTICE OF DISCLAIMER OF LEASE

(*Title*.)

Take Notice that, pursuant to an Order of the Court, dated the day of , 19 , I, the Liquidator of the above-named company, by writing under my hand bearing date the day of 19 , disclaimed all interest in the lease dated the day of 19 , whereby the premises (*a*) were demised to at a rent of £. per annum for a term of

The above-mentioned disclaimer has been filed at the office of the Registrar at (*b*)

Dated this day of 19

To Liquidator.

(address)

(*a*) Insert description of the property disclaimed.
(*b*) State address.

35A. *Notice of Meeting (General Form) and Affidavit of Postage of*
35B. *Notice*

Rules 129 & 130	(*Members and Creditors*)	*Form 75 & 76* (*R*) *WUR 76* (*J*)

No. 75. (Rule 129.)

NOTICE OF MEETING [GENERAL FORM]

(*Title.*)

Take notice that a meeting of creditors [*or* contributories] in the above matter will be held at on the day of 19 , at o'clock in the noon.

Agenda

(*a*)

Dated this day of 19

(Signed) (*b*)

Forms of general and special proxies are enclosed herewith. Proxies to be used at the meeting must be lodged with at , in the County of not later than o'clock on the day of 19

(*a*) [Here insert purpose for which meeting called.]
(*b*) "Liquidator" or "Official Receiver," or as the case may be. *See* Rule 129.

form No. WUR 76

[Rule 130 The Companies]
(Winding-up) Rules 1949,

affidavit of postage of notices of meetings

name of company

....

.... Limited

.... of ....

....

.... Description ....

make oath and say as follows:—

1. That I did on the........................day of...................19.., send to each Creditor mentioned in the Company's statement of affairs [or to each Contributory mentioned in the register of members of the Company] a notice of the time and place of the (1).. in the form hereunto annexed marked "A".

2. That the notices for Creditors were addressed to the said Creditors respectively according to their respective names and addresses appearing in the statement of affairs of the Company or the last known addresses of such Creditors.

3. That the notices for Contributories were addressed to the Contributories respectively according to their respective names and registered or last known addresses appearing in the register of the Company.

4. That I sent the said notices by putting the same prepaid into the post office at .... before the hour of..............o'clock in the..........noon on the said day.

SWORN by the above-named

....

....

this..........day of..........19.... ....

Signature of Deponent

Before me

....

(A Commissioner for Oaths)

NOTE:
(1) Insert here "general" or "adjourned" or "first" meeting of creditors [or contributories as the case may be]

36. *Notice of Return to Contributories*
Rule 120 (*Members and Creditors*) *Form 69* (*R*)

NO. 69 (Rule 120)

NOTICE OF RETURN TO CONTRIBUTORIES

(Title)

Address

Date 19

Notice is hereby given that a return of p per share has been authorised by the Court in this matter, and that the same may be received at my office, as above, on the day of 19 or any subsequent weekday, except , between the hours of and

NOTE:

(i) This form together with the share certificate must be presented, or returned, to the Liquidator when application for payment is made.
(ii) If you do not desire to attend personally you must fill up, sign and return the form of authority below, when a payable order will be delivered in accordance with the authority.
(iii) Payable orders lapse if not presented for payment within 3 months of the last day of the month of issue but will be re-issued after that period on application to the Department of Trade and Industry.

The fee payable on re-issue of a payable order is 13p where the order is for £5 or less, and 25p where the order exceeds £5.

(Signed)

Liquidator.

To ....

AUTHORITY

Sir,

Please deliver to *me (us) by post, / the Bearer, Mr. at my (our) risk the Payable Order for £ being the amount payable to *me / us in respect of the return of per share held by *me / us in this company.

£______. <u>*Contributory's signature*</u>

To the Liquidator Date 19 .

NOTE. The authority should be signed by—

(*a*) the contributory personally, or
(*b*) in the case of joint contributories, by each, or
(*c*) in the case of a firm, by one of the partners, or
(*d*) in the case of a limited company, by an officer of the company, so described, or
(*e*) in the case of a holder of a general proxy authorised to receive the dividend, by the holder.

(For use when payable order handed to creditor or representative)
Received Payable Order for £______ Signed

Date 19

* Strike out words inapplicable.

37. *List of Creditors or Contributories to be used at Every Meeting*
Rule 145(2) (*Members and Creditors*) *Form 74 (R)* *WUR 74 (J)*

form No. WUR 74

[Rule 145 (2), The Companies (Winding-up) Rules 1949]

list of creditors [or contributories]

(Delete which does not apply)

To be used at every meeting

name of company

....

.... Limited

(in voluntary liquidation)

meeting held at..

this....................day of.......................... 19....

Consecutive Number	Names of Creditors [or Contributories] present or represented	Amount of Proof*	
		In person	Proxies
		£	£
....	....	....	....
....	....	....	....
	Total number of Creditors [or Contributories] present or represented		

* NOTE: In case of Contributories insert "Number of Shares" and "Number of votes according to the regulations of the Company".

No. 84. (Rule 173.)

CERTIFICATE AND REQUEST BY COMMITTEE OF INSPECTION AS TO INVESTMENT OF FUNDS

(*Title.*)

We, the Committee of Inspection in the above matter, hereby certify that in our opinion the cash balance standing to the credit of the above-named company is in excess of the amount which is required for the time being to answer demands in respect of such company's estate, and request that the Board of Trade will invest the sum of £ in Government securities, to be placed to the credit of the said account for the benefit of the said company

Dated this day of 19

....
.... Committee of Inspection.
....

No. 85. (Rule 173.)

REQUEST BY COMMITTEE OF INSPECTION TO BOARD OF TRADE TO SELL SECURITIES

(*Title.*)

We, the Committee of Inspection in the above matter, hereby certify that a sum of £ , forming part of the assets of the above-named company, has been invested in Government Securities, and that the sum of £ is now required to answer demands in respect of the said company. And we request that so much of the said securities as may be necessary for the purpose of answering such demands may be realised by the Board of Trade, and that the amount realised may be placed to the credit of the said company.

Dated this day of 19

....
.... Committee of Inspection.
....

39. *Liquidator's Notice requiring Payment of Money, Delivery of Books, etc.*
Rule 79 (*Members and Creditors*) *Form 37* (*R*)

No. 37. (Rule 79.)

NOTICE BY LIQUIDATOR REQUIRING PAYMENT OF MONEY OR DELIVERY OF BOOKS, &c., TO LIQUIDATOR

(*Title*.)

Take notice that I, the undersigned (*a*) , have been appointed liquidator of the above-named company, and that you, the undermentioned (*b*) , are required within days after service hereof, to pay to me [*or* deliver, convey, surrender, or transfer to or into my hands] as liquidator of the said company at my office, situate at (*c*) &c., the sum of £ , being the amount of debt appearing to be due from you on your account with the said company [*or* any money, property, books or papers], [*or specifically describe the property*] now being in your hands, and to which the said company is entitled [*or otherwise as the case may be*].

Dated this day of 19 .

(Signed)

Liquidator.

To (*b*)
(*Address*)

(*a*) Name of liquidator.
(*b*) Name of person to whom notice is addressed.
(*c*) Address of liquidator's office.

40. *Resolution authorising distribution of assets in Specie*
(Members) *Specimen*

extraordinary resolution authorising distributions of assets in specie

(*a*) *All assets*
Resolved that the Liquidator be authorised to divide all or such part of the surplus assets of the Company as he shall think fit in specie amongst the members of the Company.

(b) *Specified assets*
Resolved that the Liquidator be authorised to divide in specie amongst the members of the Company in full satisfaction of their claims therein, the Company's investments in
in proportion to each member's shareholding having made such fractional adjustments thereto as he may consider necessary.

Note: Extraordinary Resolutions required by Table A, Art. 135 (if adopted).

41. *Indemnity to be given to Liquidator by those asking him to act*
(Members and Creditors) *Specimen*

Liquidator's Indemnity

To..(proposed Liquidator)
Dear Sir,

Re: A.B.C. Limited

In consideration of your agreeing to act as Liquidator of the above mentioned Company pursuant to a Resolution dated this day of . 19
WE hereby jointly and severally undertake to pay or reimburse you (as the case may require) so much of the debts expenses and liabilities properly incurred by you in the performance of your duties as Liquidator and so much of your remuneration for so acting as you are unable to recover from the moneys coming into your hands as Liquidator.

Your remuneration is to be calculated upon the following basis (namely) :—
....
....
....
....

Yours faithfully,

....

42. *Memorandum of Adjournment of Meeting*
Rule 137 (*Members and Creditors*) *Form 79* (*R*)

No. 79. (Rule 137.)

MEMORANDUM OF ADJOURNMENT OF MEETING

(*Title.*)

Before
at
on the day of , 19 , at
o'clock.

Memorandum.—The (*a*) Meeting of (*b*) in the above matter was held at the time and place above mentioned; but it appearing that (*c*) the meeting was adjourned until the day of , 19 , at o'clock in the noon, then to be held at the same place.

Chairman.

(*a*) "First" *or as t he case may be.*
(*b*) Insert "creditors" *or* "contributories", *as the case may be.*
(*c*) Here state reason for adjournment.

43. *Call*
Rule 88 (*Members and Creditors*) *Form 53* (*R*)

No. 53. (Rule 88.)

DOCUMENT MAKING A CALL

(*Title.*)

I, the [Official Receiver and] Liquidator of the above-named Company, in the pursuance of (*a*) made (*or* passed) this day of 19 , hereby make a call of per share on all the contributories of the Company, which sum is to be paid at my office (*b*)
on the day of 19

Dated this day of 19

(*a*) An order of court, *or* resolution of the Committee of Inspection
(*b*) Insert address.

Appendix 3 FEES

The Companies (Department of Trade) Fees Order 1980
(S.I. 1980 No. 2008)

This order prescribes (inter alia) the fees for the Official Receiver when acting as Liquidator in a Compulsory Winding-Up. It does not apply to a Voluntary Winding-Up, but Voluntary Liquidators may find it useful for reference purposes.

The Companies (Department of Trade) Fees Order 1980

Made – – – –	*8th December 1980*
Coming into Operation	*1st January 1981*

The Lord Chancellor and the Treasury, in exercise of the powers conferred on them by section 365(3) of the Companies Act 1948 and sections 2 and 3 of the Public Offices Fees Act 1879, hereby make, sanction and consent to the following Order:—

1.—(1) This Order may be cited as the Companies (Department of Trade) Fees Order 1980 and shall come into operation on 1st January 1981.

(2) Unless the context otherwise requires, a fee referred to by number in this Order means a fee so numbered in the Schedule to this Order.

2. The fees and percentages to be charged for and in respect of proceedings in the winding-up of companies shall be those set out in the Schedule to this Order.

3.—(1) All fees should be taken in cash.

(2) When a fee is paid to an officer of a court the person paying

the fee shall inform the officer that the fee relates to a proceeding for or in the winding-up of a company.

4. Where Value Added Tax is chargeable in respect of provision of any service for which a fee is prescribed in the Schedule, there shall be payable in addition to that fee the amount of the Value Added Tax.

5. Where the head office of the company being wound up is situated out of England, and the liquidation takes place partly in England and partly elsewhere, or where the court has sanctioned a reconstruction of the company or a scheme of arrangement of its affairs, or where for any other reason the Secretary of State is satisfied that the fees would be excessive, such reduction may be made in the said fees as may, on the application of the Secretary of State, be sanctioned by the Treasury.

6. The Companies (Department of Trade) Fees Order 1975, the Companies (Department of Trade) Fees (Amendment) Order 1976, the Companies (Department of Trade) Fees (Amendment) Order 1978, the Companies (Department of Trade) Fees (Amendment No. 2) Order 1978, the Companies (Department of Trade) Fees (Amendment No. 3) Order 1978, the Companies (Department of Trade) Fees (Amendment) Order 1979, the Companies (Department of Trade) Fees (Amendment No. 2) Order 1979 and the Companies (Department of Trade) Fees (Amendment) Order 1980 are hereby revoked save as to any fee or percentage due or payable before the commencement of this Order.

Dated 1st December 1980. *Hailsham of St. Marylebone, C.*

Dated 8th December 1980.

Peter Morrison,
David Waddington,
Two of the Lords Commissioners
of Her Majesty's Treasury

SCHEDULE

No. of fee	Description of Proceeding	Amount
		£
1	On an application to the Secretary of State under section 15 of the Companies (Winding-up) Act 1890, section 224 of the Companies (Consolidation) Act 1908, or section 343 of the Companies Act 1948 for the payment of money out of the Insolvency Services Account or for the reissue of a cheque, money order or payable order in respect of money standing to the credit of the Insolvency Services Account	2·00
2	On payments of money out of the Insolvency Services Account under section 15 of the Companies (Winding-up) Act 1890, section 224 of the Companies (Consolidation) Act 1908, or section 343 of the Companies Act 1948:	
	(1) Where the money consists of unclaimed dividends— on each dividend paid out .. .. per cent	1·25
	(2) Where the money consists of undistributed funds or balances—	
	(i) on the first £50,000 or fraction thereof per cent	1·25
	(ii) on all further amounts .. .. per cent	0·75
	but so that— (*a*) the total fee payable under this sub-paragraph shall not exceed £5,000, (*b*) this fee and Fee No. 5 shall be disregarded in calculating the fee payable under this sub-paragraph.	
3	At the due date for liquidators (including the Official Receiver when he is liquidator) sending accounts of their receipts and payments for the immediately preceding six months to the Secretary of State under section 249 of the Companies Act 1948, a fee according to the following scale on the amount paid into the Insolvency Services Account in the said six months (after deducting any sums paid to secured creditors (other than debenture holders) in respect of their securities and any sums spent out of money received in carrying on the business of the company)—	
	(*a*) on the first £50,000 or fraction thereof .. per cent	10·00
	(*b*) on the next £50,000 or fraction thereof .. per cent	7·50
	(*c*) on the next £400,000 or fraction thereof per cent	6·50
	(*d*) on the next £500,000 or fraction thereof per cent	3·75
	(*e*) on the next £4,000,000 or fraction thereof per cent	2·00
	(*f*) on all further amounts .. .. .. per cent	1·00
4	On an application by a liquidator to the Secretary of State or to an Official Receiver to exercise the powers of a Committee of Inspection under section 254 of the Companies Act 1948 and Winding-up Rule 214— for each separate item therein	15·00

No. of fee	Description of Proceeding	Amount
		£
5	On the amount expended on any purchase of Government securities (including the renewal of Treasury Bills) pursuant to a request made under section 362(1) of the Companies Act 1948 .. .. per cent	0·375
6	When the Official Receiver is provisional liquidator pursuant to section 238 of the Companies Act 1948— such amount as the Court, on the application of the Official Receiver, may consider it reasonable to direct the petitioning creditor or the company to pay to him.	
7	Where a winding-up order is made: (1) On the payments made by the Official Receiver into the Insolvency Services Account (after deducting any sums on which fees are payable under Fees Nos. 8 and 9 and any sums spent in carrying on the business of the company) a fee in accordance with the following scale—	
	(i) on the first £2,500 or fraction thereof per cent	20·00
	(ii) on the next £7,500 or fraction thereof per cent	15·00
	(iii) on the next £90,000 or fraction thereof per cent	10·00
	(iv) on all further amounts .. .. per cent	5·00
	(2) On the amount distributed in dividends or paid to preferential creditors and contributories by the Official Receiver— half of the percentage prescribed in paragraph (1) above, calculated on the amount so distributed.	
8	On the payments made by the Official Receiver into the Insolvency Services Account from the realisation of property for secured creditors (other than debenture holders)— the scale fees calculated under Fee No. 7(1) on that amount.	
9	On the payments made by the Official Receiver into the Insolvency Services Account from the realisation of property for debenture holders— the scale fees calculated under Fee No. 7(1) and (2) on that amount.	
10	For travelling, keeping possession, legal costs and other reasonable expenses of the Official Receiver— the amount disbursed.	
11	(1) For all official stationery, printing, postage and telephones— (*a*) for a number of members and creditors not exceeding 25	82·00

No. of fee	Description of Proceeding	Amount
		£
	(*b*) for every additional 10 members and creditors or part thereof	24·00
	This fee does not include the charge made by the Official Receiver or liquidator calling a meeting of creditors or contributories, for which provision is made in Rule 132 of the Companies (Winding-up) Rules 1949.	
	(2) Where the winding-up order is made on or after 18th August 1980— on the insertion in the *London Gazette* of a notice relating to a company which is being wound up by the court	13·00
	(3) Where the winding-up order was made before 1st January 1980— to cover all further insertions needed in the *London Gazette* after that date	12·00
12	Where the Official Receiver performs any duty not provided for in this Schedule, such amount as the Court, on the application of the Official Receiver with the sanction of the Secretary of State, may consider reasonable.	

Appendix 4 REGISTRAR'S NOTES

Registrar's Notes for Guidance on Voluntary Liquidation

DECLARATION OF SOLVENCY AND RESOLUTION TO WIND-UP

1. If the directors (or the majority if there are more than two) decide that the company will be able to pay its debts in full within twelve months from the commencement of the winding-up (section 283 of the Act) they should make a declaration of solvency (on form number 108). To be effective for a members' voluntary winding-up, the declaration is required (1) to be made at a meeting within five weeks immediately preceding the date of passing the resolution to wind-up the company and delivered to the Registrar of Companies for registration before the date on which such resolution is passed and (2) to embody a statement of the company's assets and liabilities as at the latest practicable date before the declaration. Otherwise the winding-up is to be treated as a creditors' voluntary winding-up.

2. If a declaration of solvency cannot be submitted for registration the winding-up must be conducted as a creditors' voluntary winding-up and the liquidator must be acceptable to the creditors (sections 293 and 294).

3. A copy of the resolution to wind-up, signed by an officer of the company or the liquidator, should be forwarded to the Registrar for registration within fifteen days of its having been passed (a typed copy on durable paper will be acceptable), and notice of his appointment should be forwarded for registration by the liquidator (on form 39C or 39D) within fourteen days of appointment. Notice of the resolution to wind-up and of the appointment of liquidator must be advertised in the London Gazette within fourteen days and should be forwarded direct to the London Gazette Office, HMSO, First Avenue House, High Holborn, London WC1. (on form 39E for notice of appointment).

4. If the winding-up continues for more than one year the liquidator should summon a general meeting of the company at the end of the first year and of each subsequent year from the commencement of the winding-up, and lay an account for that year before it (section 289 or 299). If it is a creditors' voluntary winding-up a general meeting of the creditors should also be called for that same purpose (section 299).

STATEMENTS OF RECEIPTS AND PAYMENTS

5. When a winding-up continues for more than one year the liquidator is required at the end of the first year and of every subsequent six months to forward a statement of his receipts and payments for that period to the Registrar for registration. The statement should be prepared in duplicate on form 92 (with forms 94, 95 and 96 if appropriate) and verified by affidavit on form 93 (section 342 of the Act and rules 196, 197 and 198 of the Companies (Winding-up) Rules, 1949).

RETURN OF FINAL MEETING AND DISSOLUTION

6. When the affairs of the company are fully wound-up, the liquidator should make up a full account showing how the winding-up has been conducted and the property of the company disposed of and call a general meeting of the company to lay the account before it (section 290 or 300). In the case of creditors' voluntary winding-up he should also call a meeting of the creditors for the same purpose (section 300). Notice specifying the time, place and purpose of the meeting(s) must be given in the London Gazette at least one month before the meeting. Within seven days after the meeting(s) the liquidator should forward to the Registrar a copy of the account presented to the meeting(s) (on form 110) and a return of final meeting(s) (on form 111 for a members' and on form 112 for a creditors' voluntary winding-up).

7. The company will be deemed to be dissolved three months after the return of the final meeting(s) has been registered at this office, but in certain circumstances the Court may, on application, defer the date on which dissolution takes effect.

FORMS

8. The forms mentioned may be obtained from most law stationers. Forms 108, 39C/D, 39E, 110/111 and 110/112 may be obtained also from the Registrar free.

GENERAL

9. No fees are payable for registration.

10. On request in writing the Registrar will in certain circumstances consider striking a company which is no longer carrying on business or in operation off the register under section 353 of the Act.

11. These notes are intended to serve as a guide to some of the requirements of the Companies Act, 1948 and the rules and orders made thereunder, to which reference should be made at all times. Copies of the Companies Act, 1948 may be obtained through booksellers or direct from HMSO.

12. If you are not familiar with liquidation procedure you may wish to consider putting the matter into the hands of a firm of accountants or solicitors.

Companies Registration Office,
Companies House, Crown Way, Maindy, Cardiff CF4 3UZ

Appendix 5

Regulations issued by the Secretary of State for Trade under the provisions of Rule 224 of the Companies (Winding-Up) Rules 1949[1]

DEPARTMENT OF TRADE
THE COMPANIES ACTS, 1948 TO 1976

PART I

REGULATIONS ISSUED BY THE SECRETARY OF STATE FOR TRADE UNDER THE PROVISIONS OF RULE 224 OF THE COMPANIES (WINDING-UP) RULES 1949.

1. **Remittances to Insolvency Services Account.**—All moneys received by a liquidator of a company which is being wound up by order of the court are required to be paid, without deduction, to the Insolvency Services Account at the Bank of England (unless an account with any other bank has been authorised by the Secretary of State under Section 248 of the Companies Act, 1948), and remittances are to be made once a week, or forthwith, if £400 or more has been received.

2. The remittances to the Insolvency Services Account must be accompanied by Remittance Form CD7 and CD7B and sent direct to the Bank of England, Threadneedle Street, London EC2R 8AH, by cheques drawn in favour of the 'Insolvency Services Account' and crossed 'A/c Payee only' 'Bank of England'. Forms CD7 and CD7B will be supplied on application to the Department of Trade, Insolvency Service, Centralised Accounting Unit, Williams National House, 11/13 Holborn Viaduct, London EC1A 1EL.

[1] The full text of the current regulations and of the Department of Trade Notes for Guidance of Liquidators in compulsory liquidations (issued 1st October 1977) is printed in full. It will be noted that the Regulations are applicable principally to compulsory liquidations.

3. All maturing bills of exchange must be remitted to the Insolvency Services Account accompanied by Forms CD7 and CD7B.

(Note: by Section 248(3) of the Companies Act 1948, a liquidator is absolutely prohibited from paying any sums received by him **as liquidator** into his private banking account, and by sub-section (2) as amended by the Insolvency Act 1976 it is enacted that if a liquidator at any time retains for more than ten days a sum exceeding £100 or such other amount as the Secretary of State in any particular case authorises him to retain, then unless he explains the retention to the satisfaction of the Secretary of State, he shall pay interest on the amount so retained in excess at the rate of 20% a year and shall be liable to disallowance of all or such part of his remuneration as the Secretary of State may think just, and to be removed from his office by the Secretary of State and shall be liable to pay any expenses occasioned by reason of his default. (See also General Guidance Note 4 in Part II)).

4. **Special Bank Account.**—Where a special bank account is sanctioned money received shall be paid into the appointed bank and any surplus over the limit imposed by the Secretary of State's Order must be paid into the Insolvency Services Account at the Bank of England. The bank statement(s) relating to the account must be sent at each audit date. As soon as the reason for the special bank account ceases to be operative it must be closed and the balance remitted to the Insolvency Services Account.

(Note: Under the provisions of Section 248(1) of the Companies Act, 1948 a special Bank Account will be sanctioned only if the Committee of Inspection satisfy the Secretary of State that for the purpose of carrying on the business of the company or of obtaining advances, or for any other reason, it is for the advantage of creditors or contributories that such an account be operated. The application must be made by the Committee of Inspection in Form 82 as prescribed by Rule 170 of the Companies (Winding-up) Rules 1949. If there is no Committee of Inspection a special bank account will not be authorised).

5. **Payments out of Insolvency Services Account.**—All necessary disbursements made by a liquidator on account of a company to the date of his release will be repaid to him out of any moneys standing to the credit of the company in the Insolvency Services Account on application to the Department of Trade (Form CD6). Details of the disbursements claimed must be given in the application.

Any expenses properly incurred by the liquidator but not repaid before obtaining his release, will be repaid to him by the Official Receiver out of any funds available for the purpose.

6. Cheques to the order of the payee for sums which become payable on account of the company are to be obtained by the liquidator on application by him on Form CD6 for delivery by him to the parties entitled.

(Note: In no circumstances will the Secretary of State hold himself responsible for payments made on the requisition of the liquidator).

7. **Certificate of Balance.**—The Department of Trade will certify the balance standing to the credit of a company in the Insolvency Services Account only on receipt from the liquidator of a statement of the balance shown by the bank columns of the cash book.

8. **Cash Book.**—Payments made by a liquidator shall be entered in the 'Payments' column of the cash book and the money representing those payments, which has been provided from the Insolvency Services Account, shall be entered in the 'Drawn from Bank' column.

9. Money withdrawn from the Insolvency Services Account must not be treated as receipts from realisations, but must be shown only in the 'Drawn from Bank' column of the cash book, the application of the money being entered in the 'Payments' column. Payments into the Insolvency Services Account must be shown only in the 'Paid into Bank' column in the cash book.

10. **Cancellation of Cheques and Payable Orders.**—All applications for the cancellation of cheques and payable orders are to be addressed to the Department of Trade, Insolvency Service, Centralised Accounting Unit, Williams National House, 11/13 Holborn Viaduct, London EC1A 1EL and the grounds of cancellation must be stated.

(Note: Cheques and payable orders are debited to the estate account on the date they are issued by the Department).

11. **Payment of Dividends.**—The payment of dividends will in every instance, except where a special bank account has been authorised, be made by payable orders on H.M. Paymaster-General, which will be prepared by the Department of Trade on the application of the liquidator, and will be transmitted to him for

distribution amongst the creditors. The application must be in the prescribed Form C66 and must be certified by the registrar of the court, if the proceedings are in a court other than the High Court, and by the liquidator, if the proceedings are in the High Court. In the latter case the application must be accompanied by office copies of the list of proofs filed (Rule 119(5)).

(Note: The Department of Trade will require ten working days notice to enable them to prepare the payable orders for dividends. Considerable inconvenience and extra work has been caused by liquidators transmitting imperfect and inaccurate lists of creditors, and the Department of Trade requests that great care be exercised in the preparation of them; further that in all cases of payment to executors, trustees, representative officials etc the name or names should be inserted in the list, as well as the description, eg 'A.B. and C.D., executors of E.F. deceased').

The total amount of the dividend payable is to be charged in the cash book in one sum. If the dividend has been paid by payable orders on H.M. Paymaster-General the liquidator shall destroy any lapsed payable orders on the expiration of three months from the last day of the month of issue, after first preparing a list of their numbers, names of payees, and amounts. The list shall then be forwarded to the Department of Trade, Insolvency Service, Centralised Accounting Unit, Williams National House, 11/13 Holborn Viaduct, London EC1A 1EL. On the liquidator applying for his release he must forward to the Department any unclaimed dividend payable orders which have not lapsed, and these must be defaced by cutting off the bottom right hand corner.

If the dividend is paid through a special bank, the liquidator shall, upon the declaration of a dividend, forward to the Department of Trade a certified list in Form C67 of the proofs filed (together with an office copy of the list if the proceedings are in the High Court). At the expiry of six months from the date of the declaration of the dividend the liquidator shall forward to the Department of Trade vouchers for the dividends paid and a list of those remaining unclaimed, when he will be furnished with a remittance form for payment into the Insolvency Services Account of the amount of the dividends unclaimed. Money representing unclaimed dividends must not otherwise be paid into the Insolvency Services Account.

12. **Returns to Contributories.**—Applications for payable orders for returns to contributories are to be made on Form CD6, and must be accompanied by a copy of the order of court sanctioning the return, with a schedule of contributories attached. The total amount

of each return to contributories must be entered in the Cash Book in one sum.

(Note: Liquidators are advised that before making payment of *any* liquidation moneys abroad of £5 and over the Bank of England should be consulted).

13. **Investment of Funds under Section 362 of the Companies Act 1948.**—When the cash balance standing to the credit of the account of any company is in excess of the amount which in the opinion of the Committee of Inspection is required for the time being to meet the immediate demands in respect of that company's estate the Secretary of State will, on the request of the Committee or of the liquidator if there is no Committee (in either case the request must be on Form 84), invest the amount not so required in Government securities, and the dividends on such investments will be placed to the credit of the company. When any part of the money so invested is required for the purposes of the liquidation the Department will, on the request of the Committee, or of the liquidator (in either case the request must be on Form 85), sell such part of the said securities as may be necessary.

(Note: If it is not considered desirable to invest in Government securities, it is provided by Section 362(4) that when the amount to the credit of a company's account in the hands of the Secretary of State exceeds £2,000, and the liquidator gives notice to the Secretary of State that the excess is not required for the purposes of the liquidation, the company shall be entitled to interest. The rate of interest is currently 3½ per cent per annum, but such other rate may for the time being be prescribed by the Treasury. The interest will be credited to the account of the company less income tax).

Notice under Section 362(4) must be given to the Secretary of State in writing and must be addressed to Insolvency Service, Centralised Accounting Unit, Williams National House, 11/13 Holborn Viaduct, London EC1A 1EL. Interest will accrue from the date on which notice is received by the Secretary of State.

In cases where an excess balance is earning interest and further sums are paid into the Insolvency Services Account to the credit of the company a fresh notice in writing must be given to the Secretary of State by the liquidator if it is desired that interest shall be allowed on these further sums.

14. **Procedure Prior to and on Application for Release.**—On making application to the Secretary of State for release a liquidator must submit the following:

(a) Formal application for release (Form 99).

(b) Affidavit as evidence of postage to creditors and contributories of the notice of intention to apply for release and summary of account issued therewith. (A copy of the notice and summary must be attached to the affidavit and marked as an exhibit thereto by the Commissioner before whom it is sworn).

(c) Gazette notice of release stamped with insolvency stamps value £3.[1]

(d) An additional copy of the notice and summary.

(e) A duly verified copy of the cash book, in duplicate, from the date of the last account to the date of application for release.

(Note: Rule 205(1) of the Companies (Winding-up) Rules, 1949, provides that before applying to the Secretary of State for his release, a liquidator shall send to all the creditors who have proved their debts and to each contributory a notice of his intention to apply to the Secretary of State for his release (Form 98) and shall send with this notice a summary of the receipts and payments throughout the whole period of the liquidation. (Form 100).

The forms referred to are, in each case, the forms appearing in the appendix to the Companies (Winding-up) Rules 1949.

Forms 98 and 100 may be printed and the cost charged against the estate of the company. It should be borne in mind that the footnote to Form 98 is an essential part of the form.

Form 99 may be prepared in manuscript or typed.

Forms of the documents referred to in sub-paragraphs b. c. and e. above may be obtained on application to the Department of Trade, 2/14 Bunhill Row, London EC1Y 8LL).

PART II

General Guidance Notes

1. **Employment of Solicitors under General Retainers.**—As a matter of general practice the Department of Trade consider that authorities and retainers to solicitors should be in specific terms. It is recognised, however, that in a large complex liquidation it may be an embarrassment for the liquidator to obtain specific sanction from the Court or his Committee of Inspection on each occasion that he wishes to employ a Solicitor and in those circumstances he may wish to obtain sanction to employ a Solicitor under a general retainer.

[1] Fees on insertion of individual notices in the London Gazette and Insolvency stamps were abolished under the Companies (Department of Trade) Fees (Amendment No. 2) Order 1979.

Liquidators are asked to make use of general retainers in exceptional cases only and in such cases (to ensure that no unnecessary difficulties arise on the taxation of bills) liquidators should give written instructions to the Solicitor to deal with particular matters arising which are to be covered by that general retainer. If it is necessary in a matter of urgency to give instructions orally, they should be confirmed in writing.

2. **Supply of Registration particulars of Motor Vehicles.**—As a result of the Department's representations, the Department of the Environment have instructed all local authorities that registration particulars of motor vehicles may be furnished to liquidators in cases where the information is required to establish whether they have a claim to the legal ownership of specific vehicles.

3. **Claims by Litigants legally aided.**—The Legal Aid and Advice Act 1949, provides in section 2(2)(d) that costs are to be paid into the Legal Aid Fund and not to the assisted litigant. By section 3(4) the Fund has a first charge on any property recovered or preserved for an assisted person up to the amount of the liability of the Legal Aid Fund on his account. This liability is made up of sums paid or payable on his account in respect of the proceedings to any solicitor or counsel and not recouped to the Fund by sums recovered by virtue of costs in his favour.

Regulation 18(2) of the Legal Aid (General) Regulations 1971(a) provides that with certain exceptions (see below) all moneys payable or repayable to an assisted person should be remitted to his solicitor or, if he is no longer represented by a solicitor, to the Law Society; only the solicitor or as the case may be the Law Society shall be capable of giving a good discharge for the payment so made. The payment of costs in authorised summary proceedings shall be made to the clerk to the justice who shall be able to give a discharge.

The Regulation further provides that where moneys are payable out of the property of a company in liquidation, to the solicitor of an assisted person or to the Law Society, the solicitor or the Society shall lodge with the liquidator a notice in accordance with Form 4 of the Regulation which shall operate as a request by the assisted person for payment to the solicitor or Society and shall be sufficient authority for that purpose. No further authority would be required to enable the liquidator to pay a dividend on a proof of debt already lodged by an assisted person to his solicitor or to the Society as the case may be.

The Regulation also enables the Law Society to take proceedings for the recovery of moneys payable to an assisted person and it may also prove for and receive dividends.

The exceptions referred to above relate to proceedings under certain Acts dealing with affiliation, matrimonial causes and family matters.

4. **Employment Protection Act.**—The Department of Employment has made arrangements to pay to liquidators (in their capacity as agents for that Department) monies to be distributed in respect of employees' claims under the Employment Protection Act. As these monies do *not* form part of estate funds they should *not* be paid into the Insolvency Services Account, but should be dealt with outside the liquidation.

PART III

Companies Wound Up by Order of the Court

The following regulations as to taxes have been approved by the Department of Trade and the Commissioners of Inland Revenue.

1. As regards corporation tax for which the company is liable, proof will be made for the full amount of tax assessed irrespective of the date of assessment. Such tax will rank for dividend except in so far as it is tax payable in priority under Section 319(1) of the Companies Act 1948. Proof will not be made for tax in so far as that tax falls to be treated as part of the expenses of the winding-up.

2. As regards income tax for which the company is liable for years prior to the relevant date (see Note 1(a)), proof will be made for the full amount of the tax assessed irrespective of the date of assessment. Such tax will rank for dividend except in so far as it is tax payable in priority under Section 319 of the Companies Act 1948.

3. As regards income tax for the year commencing 6 April in which the relevant date occurs—

(a) where the liability to tax arises prior to the relevant date, proof may be lodged for the tax assessed or subsequently assessed on the company;

(b) where the liability to tax arises subsequent to the relevant date, proof will not be lodged but such tax may be payable as part of the expenses of the winding-up.

4. (a) Where proof has been made for tax assessed upon the company and it is claimed that the company has no liability to tax, or that the assessments are excessive, an affidavit by the secretary or other officer of the company setting out the grounds of claim, accompanied by a certificate by the liquidator, in the terms of the first schedule to these regulations, may be submitted and upon receipt thereof the Inland Revenue authorities will forgo so much of the claim as appears to them on an examination of the said affidavit and certificate to be excessive. The form to be used for the purpose of such claim may be obtained from the Inspector of Taxes upon application.

(b) In cases where an affidavit by the secretary or other officer cannot be obtained a certificate by the liquidator may be submitted but the reason for failure to furnish an affidavit must be stated in the certificate.

(c) Any waiver of claim under this regulation shall not extend to tax which the company was entitled to deduct from any yearly interest of money, annuities, royalties or other sums paid in respect of the user of a patent or copyright, or other annual payments.

5. Where before the date of the winding-up order a Collector of Taxes has levied a distress against the goods or effects of the company but has not sold them, the following conditions will apply:

(a) If the distress was levied after the commencement of the winding-up (see Note 1(b)) the Collector will abandon the distress and will deliver to the liquidator the goods seized or if they have been sold by him the proceeds of sale. The tax in respect of which the distress was levied will be proved in the winding-up and will rank for dividend except so far as it is payable in priority under Section 319(1) of the Companies Act, 1948.

(b) If the distress was levied but not completed before the commencement of the winding-up, the Collector will, if requested by the provisional liquidator or the liquidator, withdraw upon receiving from him an undertaking, in the terms of the second schedule to these regulations, to treat such sum as may be legally due to the Collector under and by virtue of the distress levied as a charge on the goods or effects so distrained on, provided that if distress was levied within three months next before the date of the winding-up order this charge will be subject to 'the first charge' imposed by the provisions of Section 319(7) of the Companies Act, 1948.

6. The proceeds of sale of any distress levied by a Collector of Taxes within three months before the date of the winding-up order, which was completed by sale of the goods by the Collector, will be subject to the first charge imposed by Section 319(7) of the Companies Act, 1948.

Note: 1(a)—The relevant date in paragraphs (1), (2) and (3) hereof means:—

(i) in the case of a company ordered to be wound up compulsorily, the date of the appointment (or first appointment) of a provisional liquidator, or, if no such appointment was made, the date of the winding-up order unless in either case the company had commenced to be wound up voluntarily before that date: and

(ii) in any case where the foregoing sub-paragraph does not apply, means the date of the passing of the resolution for the winding-up of the company.

Note: 1(b)—In the above regulations the commencement of the winding-up is to be taken as the date of the presentation of the petition for winding-up, except in the case where a resolution was passed for voluntary winding-up prior to the presentation of such petition in which case the winding-up will be deemed to have commenced at the date of such resolution (Section 229 of Companies Act, 1948).

Note: 2 In the above regulations the reference to income tax should be treated as including any surtax where such tax has been assessed in the name of the company.

Note: 3 Similar rights of distress to those relating to tax under the PAYE scheme are applicable to national insurance contributions recoverable by a Collector of Taxes.

FIRST SCHEDULE

Claim for relief from Assessments of Corporation Tax or Income Tax

THE COMPANIES ACT, 1948

In the matter of .... Limited

of ....

I .... the .... of the

above-named company, do hereby make oath and say as follows:

That the said company is justly and truly entitled to be relieved from the payment of the sum of £ : being the corporation tax payable under the assessments for the accounting periods from .... to..and the income tax under the assessments for the year(s) from 6 April............to 5 April............on the following grounds:—

*

Sworn at
this day of
19 .

* Here specify the grounds of claim.

Before me ....

CERTIFICATE

I hereby certify that from an examination of the officers of Limited and from such evidence, books, accounts etc., as have been produced to me, it appears that if the company had availed itself on the statutory provisions for relief there would have been

*no

less liability to tax and that, therefore, the company should be relieved accordingly.

Signed ....

Liquidator

Dated this day of 19 .

Note: 1—Any waiver of claim in consequence of the above certificate will not extend to tax which the company was entitled to deduct from any interest of money, annuities, royalties or other sums paid in respect of the user of a patent or copyright, or other annual payments.

Note: 11—The evidence in support of the claim for relief should be attached to this certificate.

*Strike out as appropriate.

SECOND SCHEDULE

THE COMPANIES ACT, 1948

UNDERTAKING AS TO PAYMENT OF TAXES* [AND NATIONAL INSURANCE CONTRIBUTIONS] IN CASES OF DISTRESS.

RE .... Limited

In consideration of your forbearing to realize and withdrawing from possession under the distress which you have levied or caused to be levied upon such goods of the above-named company as are liable to a distress for taxes *[and National Insurance contributions] in arrear due from such company, I HEREBY UNDERTAKE (without prejudice to the rights of preferential creditors under Section 139(1) of the Companies Act, 1948), to treat the amount of money for which such distress is available, including the costs which you have incurred in the above levy, as a first charge on the net proceeds of any realization of such goods which may come into my hands, subject only to the rights of such preferential creditors.

Dated this day of 19 .

.... Liquidator

Address ....

....

TO: ....

....

*Omit where inappropriate.

Appendix 6 PENALTIES[1]

Table of Penalties

Subject Matter of Offence	Section or Schedule	Persons Liable	Maximum Penalty
Agreement with Creditors. Obtaining by false representations.	328(1)(p)	Past or present officer	Seven years or a fine or both
Altering or omitting entries in books or papers.	328(1)(k)	Past or present officer	Seven years or a fine or both
Body Corporate acting as Liquidator.	335(b)	Body Corporate	A fine
Books and papers. Failure to deliver to Liquidator.	328(1)(c)	Past or present officer	Seven years or a fine or both
Books and papers. Concealing, destroying, mutilating or falsifying.	328(1)(i)	Past or present officer	Seven years or a fine or both
Books and papers. Preventing production of.	328(1)(h)	Past or present officer	Seven years or a fine or both
Carrying on business fraudulently.	332(3)	Any person	Seven years or a fine or both
Credit. Obtaining by falsely representing that Company is carrying on business.	328(1)(n)	Past or present officer	Seven years or a fine or both
Credit. Obtaining by fraud.	328(1)(m)	Past or present officer	Seven years or a fine or both
Creditors' Voluntary Winding-up. Failure to call first meeting of Creditors.	293(6)	Company and every officer	A fine
Creditors' Voluntary Winding-up. Failure to call periodic and final meetings.	299(2) 300(6)	Liquidator	On summary conviction a fine not exceeding ⅓ of the statutory maximum[2]
Debts. Concealment of.	328(1)(d)	Past or present officer	Seven years or a fine or both
Declaration of Solvency. Failure of Liquidator to call meeting of Creditors if Company unable to pay debts in named time.	288(2)	Liquidator	On summary conviction a fine not exceeding ⅓ of the statutory maximum[2]
Destroying books, etc.	329	Officer or Contributory	Seven years or a fine or both
Dissolution. Failure of Liquidator to register Order	274(3)	Liquidator	On summary conviction a fine not exceeding ⅓ of the statutory maximum[2]

Document. Altering, parting with, omitting from.	328(1)(k)	Past or present officer	Seven years or a fine or both
Entry, fraudulent, in books, etc.	329	Officer or Contributory	Seven years or a fine or both
False debt. Failure to reveal proof of.	328(1)(g)	Past or present officer	Seven years or a fine or both
False entry. Making in any books or papers.	328(1)(j)	Past or present officer	Seven years or a fine or both
Fraud. By Officer of Company in liquidation.	330	Officer	Two years or a fine or both
Inducing credit.	330	Officer	Two years or a fine or both
Invoices. Orders, business letters. Failure to state that Company in liquidation.	338(2)	Officer, Liquidator, Receiver or Manager	On summary conviction a fine not exceeding ⅕ of the statutory maximum[2]
Liquidator, Accounts. Failure to register.	324(2)	Liquidator	On summary conviction a fine not exceeding ⅕ of the statutory maximum[2]
Liquidator. Appointment, failure to gazette and register Notice of.	305(2)	Liquidator	On summary conviction a fine not exceeding ⅕ of the statutory maximum[2]
Liquidator. Final meeting, failure to call.	290(6) 300(6)	Liquidator	On summary conviction a fine not exceeding ⅕ of the statutory maximum[2]
Losses or Expenses. Fictitious.	328(1)(l)	Past or present officer	Seven years or a fine or both
Omission. Material, from Statement of Affairs.	328(1)(f)	Past or present officer	Seven years or a fine or both
Property of Company. Failure to deliver to Liquidator.	328(1)(b)	Past or present officer	Seven years or a fine or both
Property of Company. Failure to reveal to Liquidator.	328(1)(a)	Past of present officer	Seven years or a fine or both
Property of Company. Fraudulent removal.	328(1)(e)	Past or present officer	Seven years or a fine or both
Property of Company, £10 and over. Concealing.	328(1)(d)	Past or present officer	Seven years or a fine or both
Receiving pawned or pledged property of Company.	328(2)	Any person	Seven years or a fine or both
Registers, Books, Documents or Securities. Destroying, mutilating, altering, falsifying.	329	Any officer or Contributory	Seven years or a fine or both
Removing property of Company fraudulently.	328(1)(e)	Past or present officer	Seven years or a fine or both
Resolution to Wind-Up. Failure to gazette.	279(2)	Company, Officer and Liquidator	On summary conviction a fine not exceeding ⅕ of the statutory maximum[2]
Statement of Affairs. Inspection, false statement by applicant.	235(7)	Any person	As for Contempt of Court
Statement of Affairs. Failure to make out.	235(5)	Any person	A fine

[1] As now provided under s.80 and Schedule 2 of the Companies Act 1980.
[2] The statutory maximum fine on summary conviction is currently £1000.

Appendix 7 THE LIQUIDATOR AND THE INLAND REVENUE

The Liquidator's activities may give rise to tax liabilities upon the company for which he is accountable. The liquidation may also give rise to tax liabilities for the members of the Company. This appendix summarises the main potential liabilities for both the Company and the members.

Liabilities of the Company

(1) *Corporation Tax Generally*

Corporation tax is a tax on the total profits of U.K. resident companies and of non-U.K. resident companies trading in the U.K. through a branch or agency.[1] "Total profits" are defined[2] to include income and chargeable gains. Gains of a capital nature are charged at a lower effective rate[3] than income profits. The charge is levied on the profits arising in a "Financial Year". That is, in a year to 31st March. So, for example, the year ending on 31st March 1981 is referred to as the 1980 financial year. Rates of corporation tax are fixed in arrears by reference to Financial Years.[4] If a company's accounting period straddles Financial Years the profits are apportioned to the respective years on a time basis.[5] The "commencement" of a winding-up[6] is treated as the end of one accounting period and the commencement of another.[7]

[1] Income and Corporation Taxes Act 1970, section 238; see also *ibid* section 246.

[2] See the definition in Income and Corporation Taxes Act 1970, section 238(4).

[3] Currently 30%; see Finance Act 1972, section 93 as amended. Special rules apply when a company is in liquidation; see Income and Corporation Taxes Act 1970, section 245.

[4] Income and Corporation Taxes Act 1970, section 238(1); see for example Finance Act 1980, section 19.

[5] Income and Corporation Taxes Act 1970, section 243(3) and section 527(11); see generally *ibid* section 247 as to accounting periods.

[6] The date of commencement is defined for this purpose by Income and Corporation Taxes Act 1970, section 247(7).

[7] See *ibid*.

(2) *Profits Earned During Liquidation*

Once the liquidation has begun the Liquidator is the "proper officer" of the Company.[1] He therefore becomes liable to make returns on behalf of the Company and is accountable for tax due by the Company. Of course, he has a right of indemnity in respect of tax which he pays personally.[2] If the Liquidator carries on the Company's trade, liabilities to corporation tax will arise if profits are earned.[3] Although a company in liquidation ceases to be a beneficial owner of its assets[4] this does not mean that it is not liable to corporation tax. Equally, capital gains arising on disposals of assets during the liquidation are chargeable in the normal way. Loss relief continues to be available. It is specifically provided that relief from corporation tax on chargeable gains is to be available on inter-group transfers even though the liquidation has commenced.[5] This prevents the destruction of the group relationship which would otherwise have occurred by reason of the normal rule that the liquidation destroys the Company's beneficial ownership of its assets.[6] Special provision is similarly made when a company leaves a group of companies by reason of that or any other company being wound up or dissolved.[7] Such an occasion does not give rise to any charge to corporation tax on chargeable gains. Without this special provision such a charge could otherwise have arisen upon a company "leaving a group".[8]

(3) *Distributions by the Liquidator*

Distributions made by the Liquidator "in respect of share capital" are not distributions for income tax purposes.[9] It follows that they

[1] Taxes Management Act 1970, section 108(3)(a).

[2] *Ibid* section 108(1), (2).

[3] Whether the Liquidator is "trading" or merely realising assets is a question of fact; *Wilson Box (Foreign Rights) Limited* v *Brice* [1936] 3 All E.R. 728; *John Mills Productions Limited* v *Mathias* (1967) 44 T.C. 441 at page 456.

[4] *I.R.C.* v *Olive Mill Limited* [1963] 1 W.L.R. 712; see also *Ayerst* v *C & K Construction Limited* [1976] A.C. 167 and *Pritchard* v *M. H. Builders (Wilmslow) Limited* [1969] 1 W.L.R. 409.

[5] See the normal rule in Income and Corporation Taxes Act 1970, section 273; see also *ibid* section 272(4).

[6] But stamp duty relief is not available under Finance Act 1930, section 42 because the "90% beneficial ownership" relationship is destroyed by the commencement of the liquidation.

[7] See note 11 above, and the cases there cited. See also the "group" definition in Income and Corporation Taxes Act 1970, section 272(1) read in conjunction with *ibid* section 532(1) and (3).

[8] See Income and Corporation Taxes Act 1970, section 278(1).

[9] See Income and Corporation Taxes Act 1970, section 233(1).

are not "qualifying distributions" and that there is no obligation upon the Liquidator or the Company to deduct Advance Corporation Tax.[1] This is so even though the sums distributed may include income accumulated out of the net profits of the Company. If distributions *in specie* are made these constitute disposals at market value of the distributed assets for the purposes of corporation tax on chargeable gains.

(4) *Apportionment of Income*

Under the Finance Act 1980, trading income of trading companies or members of a trading group is no longer liable to apportionment.[2] Investment income of close companies remains so liable. Circumstances may arise in which in strict law an amount of income could both be liable to apportionment and also bear capital gains tax on subsequent distribution of the income to the shareholders in a liquidation. In practice the Inland Revenue give concessionary relief in these circumstances.[3]

The Tax Position of the Members

(1) *Capital Gains Tax*

As mentioned above, distributions (in cash or *in specie*) by the Liquidator to members in respect of shares in the Company rank as capital in the hands of the members. Such distributions rank as part-disposals by the members of their shares.[4] If the distribution is *in specie*, then the member receiving the distribution takes as his base cost the market value of the asset at the date of distribution. Commonly there will be more than one distribution. In that event there will be more than one part-disposal by the members of their shares. If a capital distribution is "small" the amount of it is deducted from the base cost of the shares instead of being treated as the proceeds of a part-disposal.[5] In order to obviate time-consuming valuations for the purpose of applying the "part-disposal" formula,[6] the Inland Revenue in practice accept any reasonable valuation. Generally, the Revenue practice in this respect is set out in a press release published in 1972 but still in operation.[7]

[1] Finance Act 1972, section 84.
[2] Finance Act 1980, section 44 and Schedule 9.
[3] Inland Revenue Statement of Practice, 18th January 1977. See [1977] S.T.I. 12.
[4] Capital Gains Tax Act 1979, section 72(1).
[5] *Ibid* section 72(2).
[6] Laid down in *ibid*, section 35.
[7] Inland Revenue Press Release, published 20th January 1972.

(2) *Income and Corporation Taxes Act 1970, Section 460*

If section 460 of the Income and Corporation Taxes Act 1970 applies one result can be to render distributions to members in a liquidation chargeable as income of the recipient members. Of itself a liquidation is probably not a "transaction in securities".[1] But it can be combined with such a transaction to produce this unfortunate income treatment.[2] Before liquidating a company it will therefore be prudent to consider whether or not a prior Inland Revenue clearance should be sought.[3]

[1] Although this is not completely clear. See *I.R.C.* v *Joiner* [1975] 1 W.L.R. 1701, per Lord Wilberforce at pages 1707 to 1708; see Income and Corporation Taxes Act 1970, section 460(1)(b).

[2] *Ibid* section 460(2).

[3] There is a statutory clearance procedure under Income and Corporation Taxes Act 1970, section 464.

Index